Social Issues
in Literature

W9-AUK-330

Women's Issues in
Amy Tan's
The Joy Luck Club

Other Books in the Social Issues in Literature Series:

Class Conflict in F. Scott Fitzgerald's *The Great Gatsby*

Racism in Harper Lee's *To Kill a Mockingbird*

Racism in Maya Angelou's *I Know Why the Caged Bird Sings*

Social Issues
in Literature

Women's Issues in Amy Tan's *The Joy Luck Club*

Gary Wiener, Book Editor

GREENHAVEN PRESS

An imprint of Thomson Gale, a part of The Thomson Corporation

THOMSON

™

GALE

Detroit • New York • San Francisco • New Haven, Conn. • Waterville, Maine • London

THOMSON

GALE

™

Christine Nasso, *Publisher*
Elizabeth Des Chenes, *Managing Editor*

© 2008 The Gale Group.

For more information, contact:
Greenhaven Press
27500 Drake Rd.
Farmington Hills, MI 48331-3535
Or you can visit our Internet site at http://www.gale.com

Cover photograph reproduced by permission of Kris Timken.

ISBN-13: 978-0-7377-3898-8 (hardcover)
ISBN-10: 0-7377-3898-7 (hardcover)
ISBN-13: 978-0-7377-3902-2 (pbk.)
ISBN-10: 0-7377-3902-9 (pbk.)

Library of Congress Control Number: 2007938436

Contents

Introduction   **9**

Chronology   **12**

Chapter 1: Background on Amy Tan

1. The Life of Amy Tan   **16**

   Laurie Champion

   Driven by her demanding immigrant Asian mother, Amy Tan parlayed her early vocation as a technical writer into a career as one of the major voices in Asian American fiction by writing of the mother-daughter conflicts she experienced during her youth.

2. Tan Turns Autobiography into Powerful Fiction   **25**

   Amy Ling

   Amy Tan used material mined from her own life to create the mother-daughter tales of *The Joy Luck Club*, crafting a powerful tale of tragedy and reconciliation.

3. *The Joy Luck Club* Is Not Strictly Autobiographical   **35**

   Amy Tan

   Tan's writings are not autobiographical in the sense that many readers expect. Her stories are not childhood memories, but instead are written through the lens of a child's mind.

Chapter 2: *The Joy Luck Club* and Women's Issues

1. Tan's Young Women Must Rediscover Their Chinese Identity   **41**

   Walter Shear

   A major theme in *The Joy Luck Club* is that of being lost. The younger women must reconnect with their lost Chinese roots in order to achieve selfhood.

2. June's Symbolic Journey to Discover   **51**
Her Ethnic Identity
Zenobia Mistri

June Woo's China journey to meet her mother's daughters serves as a metaphor for all ethnic women who must affirm, rather than reject, their cultural heritage.

3. Damaged by Their Mothers' High Expectations   **60**
Wendy Ho

The mothers in *The Joy Luck Club*, having all experienced hardship and loss, place high expectations on their daughters, who are unequal to the task, and become victims of their mother's lofty goals.

4. Storytelling Reconciles Mothers and Daughters   **70**
Gloria Shen

As immigrant mothers and second-generation American daughters grow further apart, the mothers use stories to bridge the generation gap and help the daughters understand their mothers' actions as well as their cultural heritage.

5. The Maternal Line of Descent Dominates   **80**
The Joy Luck Club
Helena Grice

In *The Joy Luck Club*, as in many contemporary women's Asian American novels, matrilineage, or the maternal line of descent in a family, is a major theme.

6. Mother/Daughter Relationships   **88**
in the Post Women's Liberation Era
Bonnie Braendlin

Early feminist novels appearing in the wake of the women's liberation movements suggested rebellious ways for women to gain freedom, but novels such as *The Joy Luck Club* assert that through dialogism, women can resolve complicated issues.

7. Female Empowerment in *The Joy Luck Club*   **94**
Patricia P. Chu

Tan blends the mother-daughter romance with the utopian myth of immigration to form a tale of female empowerment in a new world.

8. Tan's Beginning Rejects Stereotypes   100
About Immigrant Women
Catherine Romagnolo

The opening of *The Joy Luck Club* has been criticized for distorting Chinese culture, but Tan's book is consciously an attempt to counter traditional stereotypes about Asian immigrant women.

9. Empowerment Through   109
Woman-to-Woman Bonding
Leslie Bow

The Joy Luck Club upholds the feminist notion that women can become empowered through bonding with other women.

10. Asian American Gender Stereotypes   120
in *The Joy Luck Club*
Yuan Shu

Ethnic writers must be careful of the consequences of their writing strategies, as certain details in *The Joy Luck Club* may reinforce negative cultural stereotypes about Asian American men and women.

11. Tan Portrays Strong Asian Women   127
Jean Lau Chin

The Joy Luck Club's popularity among Chinese Americans owes in part to its depiction of strong Asian women, as opposed to Western stories that often depict Asian women in meek, subservient roles.

Chapter 3: Contemporary Perspectives on Women's Issues

1. Mothers Are Society's Scapegoats   136
Paula Caplan

Mothers are usually blamed for all of their children's problems, while fathers often escape such criticism.

2. Asian American Women Must Overcome   144
   Limiting Cultural Stereotypes
   Nikki A. Toyama

   Asian American women are so much more than the domestic servants that cultural stereotypes would have
   people believe.

3. Biculturalism Leads to One Woman's   150
   Acceptance of Bisexuality
   Beverly Yuen Thompson

   The "otherness" of being a racially bifurcated woman has
   made one woman's acceptance of bisexuality seem less
   radical than it might otherwise be.

4. Asian Women Are Still Not Completely   164
   Accepted in the United States
   Iris Chang

   Despite the remarkable success of many Asian-American
   women, full acceptance into mainstream American society is slow in coming.

5. More Women are Working, but Job Equality   168
   Remains Elusive
   International Labour Organization (ILO)

   Societal views of women in the workplace are changing,
   but men continue to garner more prestige and income
   than their female counterparts.

6. Feminism Is Not Dead, Just Evolving   174
   Eleanor Holmes Norton

   Young women may not consider themselves feminists,
   but the opportunities they have are based on a movement that still exists in the everyday choices and lives of
   today's women.

For Further Discussion   182

For Further Reading   184

Bibliography   185

Index   188

Introduction

Given the success of minority women authors, including African Americans such as Nobel laureate Toni Morrison (*Beloved*) and Alice Walker (*The Color Purple*); Asian Americans such as Maxine Hong Kingston (*The Woman Warrior*) Amy Tan and Lisa See (*Snow Flower and the Secret Fan*); Jewish Americans such as Ayn Rand (*The Fountainhead*), Erica Jong (*Fear of Flying*) and Myla Goldberg (*Bee Season*); and Arab Americans such as Azar Nafisi (*Reading Lolita in Tehran*) and poet Naomi Shihab Nye, it may come as a surprise that serious women's literature is a fairly new trend. In 1855, the American novelist Nathaniel Hawthorne bemoaned the lack of worthy women writers, claiming that "America is now wholly given over to a . . . mob of scribbling women, and I should have no chance of success while the public taste is occupied with their trash." For Hawthorne and his male contemporaries, books about women's issues were of dubious worth. Even in the early twentieth century, women's novels that are now regarded as classics, including Kate Chopin's *The Awakening* (1899) and Zora Neale Hurston's *Their Eyes Were Watching God* (1937) were subjected to harsh reviews and allowed to go out of print for decades.

But in the 1960s, society began to change in earnest, as what is now referred to as second-wave feminism began to sweep not only through the United States, but through much of the western world. The notions of women's liberation and feminism became commonplace, groups such as NOW (the National Organization for Women) and Planned Parenthood championed women's issues, women's studies programs began to spring up on college campuses everywhere, and women's literature, written for women by women, underwent a renaissance unlike anything seen before.

Amy Tan has said that the publication of her first book, *The Joy Luck Club* (1989), came at a particularly auspicious time, when baby boom mothers had daughters of their own to contend with. The book "hit a nerve because women had begun to think about themselves and their mothers." Driven in part by this new interest in matrilineage, or the maternal line of descent in a family, *The Joy Luck Club* became that rarest of books: like Harper Lee's *To Kill a Mockingbird* and Ken Kesey's *One Flew Over the Cuckoo's Nest*, or, more recently, Khaled Hosseini's *The Kite Runner*, it was a first novel phenomenon, a book that pleased both general readers and found equal favor with critics of serious literature. Suddenly Tan became the spokeswoman for not only a generation or two of American postfeminist women, but for Asian American women as well. It was pretty heady stuff for an author whose previous writing credits totaled two published short stories.

But America was certainly ready for *The Joy Luck Club*. The hardcover edition stayed on the *New York Times* best seller list for thirty-four weeks and Ivy Books paid well over a million dollars for the paperback rights. *The Joy Luck Club* was translated into twenty-five languages, but, ironically, sold poorly in China. Clearly, *The Joy Luck Club*, for all of its characters' Asian ethnicity, was a very American book.

The Joy Luck Club tells the story of eight women, all Chinese Americans, including four sets of mother-daughter pairings. Each mother, driven by cultural mores, expects the world from her daughter. Each daughter, a product of post–World War II feminist thinking, rebels from the mother in her own way. The book traces the history of these mother-daughter conflicts, and how they are ultimately and symbolically resolved by the protagonist, June (Jing-mei) Woo, in the book's final chapter.

With its focus on strong Asian American women, *The Joy Luck Club* overcame stereotypes that had been in place for centuries, even millennia. Asian culture traditionally minimized women's roles in the family and in society, at best portraying Asian women as subservient homemakers, often of polygamist husbands, or, at worst, as servants and concubines. One has to look no further than the early-twentieth-century classic about China, *The Good Earth* by Pearl Buck, the play *Madame Butterfly*, or its update, *Miss Saigon*, to see this quintessentially marginalized and long-suffering Asian woman at the mercy of forces and institutions far beyond her control. Thus it is surprising and refreshing to find that in *The Joy Luck Club*, it is men who play supporting roles, and women who act out the archetype of questing hero, searching for wholeness and a stable identity in a culture that has divided them into "Asian Americans."

Amy Tan followed *The Joy Luck Club* with a number of successful novels, the most prominent of which are *The Kitchen God's Wife* and *The Bonesetter's Daughter*. All explore the relationships of mothers and daughters, the status of Asian Americans, and women's issues in general. But *The Joy Luck Club* remains her signature book, one which not only enabled her to break onto the literary scene, but which paved the way for subsequent Asian American literary works by women in the late twentieth and early twenty-first centuries.

The articles that follow place *The Joy Luck Club* in the context of women's issues, demonstrating why a first book by a complete unknown took the literary world by storm. They also suggest the nearly universal critical support Tan received for *The Joy Luck Club* and why the book has become not only a staple of minority women's fiction, but of women's fiction in general.

Chronology

1924
Daisy Du Ching, the author's mother, is born in China.

1949
Tan's mother leaves China; she marries John Tan.

1952
Amy Tan is born on February 19 in Oakland, California.

1967
Peter Tan, Tan's brother, dies of a brain tumor.

1968
John Tan dies of a brain tumor.

1969
Tan graduates from high school in Montreux, Switzerland.

1970
She enrolls in Linfield College in Oregon.

1972
Tan transfers to San José University in California.

1973
She graduates from San José University with a B.A.

1974
Tan receives her M.A. from San José University.

1976
Tan marries Lou DeMattei. She works for Alameda County Association for Retarded Citizens as a language development consultant.

1981

Tan becomes editor of a medical journal.

1983

She becomes a freelance business writer.

1987

Tan visits China with her mother.

1989

Tan publishes *The Joy Luck Club*.

1991

Tan publishes *The Kitchen God's Wife*.

1992

Tan publishes the children's book *The Moon Lady*. She forms the band The Rock Bottom Remainders with writers such as Stephen King and Dave Barry.

1993

The film of *The Joy Luck Club*, directed by Wayne Wang, is released in theaters.

1994

Tan publishes the children's book *The Chinese Siamese Cat*.

1995

Tan publishes *The Hundred Secret Senses*.

2001

Tan publishes *The Bonesetter's Daughter*.

2003

Tan publishes *The Opposite of Fate: A Book of Musings*.

2005

Tan publishes *Saving Fish from Drowning.*

Social Issues
in Literature

CHAPTER 1

| Background on Amy Tan

The Life of Amy Tan

Laurie Champion

Laurie Champion has taught at San Diego State University. She is the editor of American Women Writers, 1900–1945: A Bio-Bibliographical Critical Sourcebook, *and, with Rhonda Austin, coeditor of* Contemporary American Women Fiction Writers: An A-to Z Guide.

Amy Tan, one of the premier voices in contemporary Asian American women's fiction, is a product of her mother's high expectations. Tan often writes of mother-daughter relationships in her fiction, focusing on the conflicts that result between those of different generations. Her novel, The Joy Luck Club, *a linked series of stories about mothers and daughters, was highly successful and launched her professional career. She followed that novel with several others, including* The Kitchen God's Wife, The Hundred Secret Senses, *and* The Bonesetter's Daughter, *all of which explore Asian American women's roles in contemporary society. Her novels have found favor with both scholars and general readers, and she is a major voice in contemporary American writing.*

Amy Tan is one of the most significant contemporary Asian American women writers. Her novels have received both critical and popular success, and she is among the first women writers to bring Asian American culture and experiences to a broad mainstream audience. Tan's works, which focus on Chinese who have immigrated to the United States, illustrate the difficulties of maintaining a dual cultural identity. Many of the struggles and conflicts her characters experience, however, transcend cultural differences. Her novels also provide a feminist view of ethnic Americans: frequently, her characters overcome obstacles that face them as minority women in racist and sexist societies. Tan's works also deal with familial bonds, usually mother-daughter relationships, and conflicts between the generations that are precipitated by cultural as well as age gaps. Although her fiction is not strictly autobiographical, many of the situations and themes spring from incidents in her life; others are based on anecdotes she heard from relatives.

Pressured to Excel

The second of three children, Amy Ruth Tan, whose Chinese name is An-mei (Blessing from America), was born on 19 February 1952 in Oakland, California. Her father, John Yueh-han Tan, an electrical engineer and Baptist minister, had immigrated to the United States in 1947; her mother, Daisy Tu Ching Tan, a vocational nurse, had immigrated in 1949. The family moved frequently among various California cities, eventually settling in Santa Clara. Like many of the mothers and daughters in Tan's novels, Tan and her mother had a strained relationship. Tan's mother had high expectations for her, and Tan felt pressure to excel. Also, her mother's attire and accent embarrassed Tan as a child and adolescent.

When Tan was fifteen, her older brother, Peter, and then her father both died of brain cancer; her mother, believing the house to be evil-spirited, took Tan and her brother John to New York, Washington, and Florida and finally to Europe. After Tan graduated from high school in Montreux, Switzerland, the family returned to the United States and settled in the San Francisco area. Tan switched from a premed major to English at Linfield College, a Baptist school in Oregon, and later transferred to San Jose State University in California. She earned a B.A. in English and linguistics in 1973 and a master's degree in linguistics in 1974. On 6 April 1974 she married Louis M. DeMattei, a tax attorney. She began work on a doctorate at the University of California, Berkeley, but left the university in

1976 to take a position as a language-development specialist for disabled children. Frustrated with the administrative aspects of the job, in 1981 she became a reporter for the journal *Emergency Room Reports* (now *Emergency Medicine Reports*), rising to managing editor and associate publisher. In 1983 she became a freelance technical writer, producing pamphlets and other documents for corporations.

Becoming a Writer

Although highly successful as a technical writer, Tan found that she had become a workaholic; when counseling failed to remedy the condition, she decided to cure herself by learning to play jazz piano and reading fiction by authors such as Alice Munroe, Flannery O'Connor, Louise Erdrich, and Amy Hempel. Her short story "The Rules of the Game" gained her admission to the Squaw Valley Community of Writers, directed by the novelist Oakley Hall; she later incorporated it into her first novel, *The Joy Luck Club* (1989). At the workshop she met Hempel and Molly Giles, who helped her to shape her talent and find her voice.

Tan's reconciliation with her mother occurred when the mother revealed her past to Tan—a past that was similar to that of characters in *The Joy Luck Club* and Tan's second novel, *The Kitchen God's Wife* (1991). In 1987 Tan and her husband traveled to China with her mother to meet two of the three daughters Daisy Tan had left behind when she fled her disastrous first marriage and immigrated to the United States. Tan had left an outline for *The Joy Luck Club* with a literary agent, Sandra Dijkstra, who sold the book to G. P. Putnam's Sons while Tan was out of the country. The novel was published in 1989.

The Joy Luck Club

The Joy Luck Club consists of sixteen interrelated short stories, told by various narrators, that move back and forth in time; the events related in the earlier stories take on new significance when the subsequent stories are read. The nonlinear narration allows the novel to progress thematically and to be driven by character development rather than plot. The main characters are four immigrant women from China and their American-born daughters: Suyuan and Jing-mei (June) Woo, An-mei Hsu and Rose Hsu Jordan, Lindo and Waverly Jong, and Ying-ying and Lena St. Clair. The novel is divided into four sections, each comprising four stories; each section is prefaced by a myth related to the four stories in it. The first and fourth sections consist of the mothers' stories, the second and third the daughters'. Each character, except Suyuan, tells her own story in the first person; since Suyuan has died two months before the novel opens, June narrates her mother's stories.

The opening chapter is narrated by June. June's father asks her to take her mother's place in the Joy Luck Club, which her mother started forty years previously, in 1949. The club is a social group in which the immigrant women meet to play mah-jongg, eat, and tell stories; it has offered the women their only joy. The three older women try to persuade June to travel to China and tell the twin half sisters she has never met about Suyuan. When June protests that she herself knows little about her mother, the other mothers are horrified:

> In me, they see their own daughters, just as ignorant, just as unmindful of all the truths and hopes they have brought to America. They see daughters who grow impatient when their mothers talk in Chinese, who think they are stupid when they explain things in fractured English. They see that joy and luck do not mean the same to their daughters, that to these closed American-born minds "joy luck" is not a word, it does not exist. They see daughters who will bear grandchildren born without any connecting hope passed from generation to generation.

The thread linking the stories is June's pursuit of knowledge about her mother so that she can tell Suyuan's story to her half sisters.

The middle sections of the novel show the mothers and daughters coming to understand and appreciate each other. Lacking opportunities in their own lives, the mothers wanted the daughters to realize the American dream while remaining connected to their Chinese heritage; the daughters felt pressured to achieve the unrealistic goals their mothers set for them. Lindo's incessant bragging to strangers about Waverly's junior chess championship led Waverly to scream that Lindo should play chess herself rather than live vicariously through her daughter; Suyuan wanted June to be a child prodigy and play the piano on *The Ed Sullivan Show*. The daughters' feeling that they could never live up to their mothers' expectations continue in adulthood: Lena's fear of how her mother will react to the house she has renovated turns out to be well founded: Ying-ying points out the flaws in the house rather than recognizing the artistic merits.

Mothers Telling Stories in *The Joy Luck Club*

The mothers tell stories about their own mothers in narratives that layer the stories their daughters tell about them. An-mei's mother became a concubine when An-mei was four; An-mei and her younger brother were raised by their grandmother, who refused to let the children talk about their mother. June narrates her mother's story as she heard it from Suyuan: Suyuan was married to an officer in the Nationalist Chinese political party; at the time of the Japanese invasion the husband left Suyuan and their twin daughters in Kweilin, where she organized the first Joy Luck Club as a haven for women to escape fear of war. Although Suyuan usually stopped telling June about her past at this point, she sometimes continued; but the conclusions of the story were inconsistent. She never explained what happened to the children. The immigrants'

Amy Tan at the 2002 "New Yorker" festival. Laurence Lucier/Getty Images.

stories describe the social codes and roles imposed on Chinese women; although they recognize the faults of the patriarchal society, the mothers still value Chinese customs and wish to teach the daughters their heritage.

The daughters, on the other hand, want to assimilate into mainstream America; sometimes they try to look more "American" to escape racist taunts. The daughters' struggles with their dual cultural identities frequently take the form of an inability to communicate with their mothers. June's mother often failed to answer her questions directly and sometimes gave her answers that were foolish superstitions: "these kinds of explanations made me feel my mother and I spoke two different languages, which we did." She talked to her mother in English and was answered in Chinese, but the lack of communication transcended linguistic barriers: June acknowledges that she and Suyuan "never really understood one another. We translated each other's meaning and I seemed to hear less than what was said, while my mother heard more." Ying-ying corrects Lindo for addressing June by her Chinese name, explaining that "They all go by their American names." As the daughters mature, however, they learn through the teaching and example of their mothers to appreciate their Chinese heritage.

As immigrants, the mothers struggle with culture shock rather than with the issues of dual identity that challenge their daughters. Rose relates that her mother believes children are susceptible to dangers on specific days related to their Chinese birthdays; An-mei is, however, unable to translate the Chinese dates into American ones. Lindo was also unable to translate dates when she wanted to choose the right day to immigrate to San Francisco. This inability to translate dates points symbolically to the loss of a sense of time and place that the women experienced on abruptly leaving one culture and entering another.

Favorable Reviews for a Feminist Novel

In addition to exploring relationships between mothers and daughters, *The Joy Luck Club* addresses male-female relationships from a feminist viewpoint. Lindo escaped from an arranged marriage in which she was unable to make choices for herself. Ying-ying's first marriage was also an arranged one, although she was in love with her husband; when he left her she married Clifford St. Clair, who loves her almost obsessively and speaks for her instead of allowing her to express herself. Lena divorced her husband, a miser who had extramarital affairs. Rose is unable to assert herself and allows her Caucasian husband, Ted, whom she married despite his mother's racist views, to make all the decisions. While the novel depicts women as victims of sexism, it also shows mothers and daughters learning from one another how to free themselves from stifling marriages.

At the end of *The Joy Luck Club* June arrives in China. By meeting her half sisters she comes to understand her mother in a way she could not have done otherwise, and the twins are linked to their mother, whom they never knew, through meeting June. "And now I also see what part of me is Chinese. It is so obvious. It is my family. It is in our blood. And although we don't speak, I know we all see it: Together we look like our mother. Her same eyes, her same mouth, open in surprise to see, at last, her long-cherished wish": her twin daughters will hear her story, and all three of her daughters will be united.

The Joy Luck Club received almost unanimously favorable reviews; it was nominated for the *Los Angeles Times* Book Award, was a finalist for the National Book Award and the National Book Critics Circle Award, and won the Bay Area Book Reviewers Award for Best Fiction, the Commonwealth Club Gold Award, and the American Library Association Best Book for Young Adults Award. It remained on *The New York Times* hardcover best-seller list for nine months—longer than any other book that year—and sold more than four million copies. It has been translated into twenty-five languages, including Chinese. Chapters from the novel appear in anthologies used in high-school and college English courses.

Tan Turns Autobiography into Powerful Fiction

Amy Ling

Amy Ling has taught at Cheng-kung University in Taiwan, Rutgers, the State University of New Jersey, and Georgetown University. She is the author of Between Worlds: Women Writers of Chinese Ancestry, *from which this excerpt is taken.*

Amy Tan uses material mined from her own life to create the mother-daughter tales of The Joy Luck Club. *When she was a teenager, Tan lost both her brother and her father to brain tumors. Her mother, fearing that their California home was responsible, moved the family to Switzerland, where Tan attended school. Later in her life, Tan endured another tragedy when a close friend was murdered. The various deaths in* The Joy Luck Club *are Tan's attempt to dramatize a world in which womankind's inevitable fate is tragic. Tan's stormy relationship with her own mother also figures into the plot of the novel, as each of the four daughters struggles to come to terms with strong, demanding matriarchs. Tan's message is that the daughters must learn to balance the old Chinese ways of their mothers with the newer American ways, as she herself had to learn to do.*

Amy Tan's *The Joy Luck Club* . . . often takes a sympathetic stand toward the mother. Though all the stories of *The Joy Luck Club* mothers are poignant, the most affecting one is Suyuan Woo's. She had been forced to leave behind twin baby girls when she was running away on foot, in panic and exhaustion, from Japanese soldiers during World War II. In the clothes of these babies, she hid jewels to pay for their care, her photograph, name, and the address of her family in Shanghai so that the babies could later be returned. But her house was bombed, her family totally annihilated, and all her efforts to recover her children were in vain. For 40 years, from America, she tried to find these lost daughters in China; at last, they were found and wrote to her, but not before her sudden death. Her daughter Jing-mei is asked to go to China to tell these sisters whom she has never met all about their mother. These sisters live in the motherland that Jing-mei has never known, and Jing-mei has lived with the mother that the sisters have never known. But when Jing-mei is first asked by her mother's friends from the Joy Luck Club to go to China on this mission, her immediate response is bewilderment: "What will I say? What can I tell them about my mother? I don't know anything. She was my mother."

The Absent Mother

Tan's implication is clear: we all take our mothers (and motherlands) for granted. They are just there, like air or water, impossible really to know or understand because we are so intimate, and more often than not they have seemed a force to struggle against. Not until they are gone do we give them any thought. Ying-ying St. Clair realizes this truth in regard to her Amah or Nanny, the mother-figure in her childhood: "Amah loved me better than her own . . . But I was very spoiled because of her; she had never taught me to think about her feelings. So l thought of Amah only as someone for my comfort, the way you might think of a fan in the summer or a heater in the winter, a blessing you appreciate and love only when it is no longer there."

By extension of this analogy, the absent motherland looms large on the horizon of the emigrant mothers whose "unspeakable tragedies left behind in China," recorded and recounted in vivid detail in *The Joy Luck Club*, resonate in their daughters, Amy Tan herself being one of the daughters. Some of the elements of Tan's life have been incorporated into her novel. A comparison of her life and her novel will enable us to see the extent that Tan has reshaped her materials into fiction.

Tan's Biography and Her Fiction

Amy Tan was born in Oakland, California, in 1952; her parents had emigrated from China in 1949, leaving behind three young daughters. They had planned to find a place to live first and then send for the daughters, but the Communist Revolution prevented their carrying out this plan. Despite years of effort on her mother's part, contact was lost. Not until Amy was 12 did she learn of the existence of these sisters. The lost, absent daughters haunted the mother, in whose mind they became the perfect, good daughters, and their example was raised aloft to haunt Amy Tan, the bad, present daughter. "A few years ago, we found them," says Amy Tan in an interview with Susan Kepner. "It was an incredible experience. We met them in China, and now one of them is here. They write to me in Chinese, and my mother reads the letters to me."

Amy Tan's life has been marked by death and change. When Amy was 15, her 16-year-old brother died of a brain tumor, the following year, her engineer-Baptist-minister father also died of a brain tumor. Her grief-stricken mother, believing that their house in Santa Clara was imbalanced in *feng shui* (wind and water), fled with her two remaining children to Switzerland, where Amy attended the College Monte Rosa Internationale in Montreux and from which she nearly eloped with an escaped mental patient who claimed to be a German army deserter. Back in the United States, she completed her bachelor's and master's degrees in English and linguistics at San Jose State University, where she met her husband, Lou DeMattei, now a tax attorney. She studied one year toward a PhD in linguistics at the University of California at Berkeley, but the sudden murder of a close friend brought to the fore all the grief and anger over the deaths of her father and brother that she had suppressed for five years. She dropped her studies and took a position as a language development specialist working with handicapped children, where she was rewarded by what she considered a miracle: a two-year-old blind boy who had never spoken spoke to her. She then took up freelance writing and joined a writing group out of which *The Joy Luck Club* grew.

When visiting a Buddhist retreat in Marin County once with her husband, Amy Tan was amazed to see so many people "trying to learn how to act Chinese. . . . I couldn't help thinking, 'If you really want to learn how to act Chinese, go live with a Chinese mother for twenty years. Then you'll act Chinese.'" What she heard from her Chinese mother for 20 years boiled down to three precepts: "First, if it's too easy, it's not worth pursuing. Second, you have to try harder, no matter what other people might have to do in the same situation— that's your lot in life. And if you're a woman, you're supposed to suffer in silence." Tan adds that she was never good at the last precept. She further explains that Chinese mothers map out your life and won't take no for an answer. If you tell them to "'shut up' you could be held as an accessory to your own murder. Or worse . . ." to their suicide. "So the ground rule is, *there is no way the daughter wins.*"

Turning Life into Fiction

The Joy Luck Club has clearly been inspired by two forces in Amy Tan's life: her relationship with her mother and the loss of loved ones through death. Tan fictionalizes the circumstances, but gives expression to the emotional trauma of the death of a loved one in Rose Hsu Jordan's story, "Half and Half." Rose, then 14 and the middle child of seven, had been asked to watch her younger brothers during a family outing at the beach. Though she sees her smallest brother, four-year-old Bing, slip off the reef into the water, she is paralyzed into shocked silence. His body never emerges. But, curiously, the story is not focused on her guilt, though she certainly is filled with it; the focus is on her mother's pain, on her fierce but futile efforts to change fate and to recover her son through her faith in God and her will power. Though her mother performs uncanny acts, like driving the family car (when she had never driven before) back along the dangerous road to the beach the next day, she is unable to bring back her son, and thereafter loses her faith in God.

By transferring her own father's death to the mother in her novel, Tan decidedly centers her book on women, and further heightens the emotional intensity of the mother/daughter bond/bondage. In life, the mother/daughter relationship disintegrates into a battle for power/autonomy, and Tan's imagination is fertile in portraying the variety of battle tactics whether it is Waverly Jong's anger at her mother's pride in her success at chess—"Why do you have to use me to show off? If you want to show off, then why don't you learn to play chess"— Jing-mei Woo's desire during her piano recital to expose the ridiculousness of her mother's desire for a concert pianist daughter—"I was determined to put a stop to her foolish pride."

Though the mothers all have different names and individual stories, they seem interchangeable in that the role of mother supersedes all other roles and is performed with the utmost seriousness and determination. . . . [A]ll the mothers in *The Joy Luck Club* are strong, powerful women. . . . Yingying St. Clair [is] a tiger, whose first husband told her, "Yingying, you have tiger eyes. They gather fire in the day. At night they shine golden." Ying-ying, with the cunning of a tiger, uses the camouflage of her stripes to lie in wait between the trees, hiding her power and ferocity until the time is ripe:

> So this is what I will do. I will gather together my past and look. I will see a thing that has already happened. The pain that cut my spirit loose. I will hold that pain in my hand until it becomes hard and shiny, more clear. And then my fierceness can come back, my golden side, my black side. I

Amy Tan and her dog Bubba, in her apartment in New York City's Soho section, October 12, 2005. AP Images.

will use this sharp pain to penetrate my daughter's tough skin and cut her tiger spirit loose. She will fight me, because this is the nature of two tigers. But I will win and give her my spirit, because this is the way a mother loves her daughter.

The mother/daughter relationship is clearly a painful one; an overt battle between two equally strong forces in which the mother uses the pain of her past experience both to "cut loose" the spirit of her daughter and to instill in the daughter the mother's own spirit. The daughter will struggle because she is also a tiger and fiercely independent, fighting against invasion, even from her own mother.

Inevitable Tragedy

In the deeply affecting story "Magpies," An-mei Hsu tells how her mother sacrificed herself, embracing the pain of her existence by commiting suicide, but carefully planning her death so that her daughter would be the beneficiary. The mothers are so strong that they endure all manner of pain to enforce their will, to show their love. The daughters, equally strong, find ways to rebel, if not openly then in secret. Even in dreams, the battle of wills does not cease, for example, in Rose Hsu's dream:

> I came to a giant playgound filled with row after row of square sandboxes. In each sandbox was a new doll. And my mother, who was not there but could see me inside out, told Old Mr. Chou [guardian of the door to dreams] she knew which doll I would pick. So I decided to pick one that was entirely different.
>
> "Stop her! Stop her!" cried my mother. As I tried to run away, Old Mr. Chou chased me, shouting, "See what happens when you don't listen to your mother!" And I became paralyzed, too scared to move in any direction.

Jing-mei's self-protective strategy against the mother who expected her to be a child prodigy is to disappoint her mother whenever possible: "I failed her so many times, each time asserting my own will, my right to fall short of expectations. I didn't get straight A's. I didn't become class president. I didn't get into Stanford. I dropped out of college." . . .

The daughters' battles for independence from powerful, commanding, mothers is fierce, but eventually . . . a reconciliation is reached. The daughters realize that the mothers have always had the daughter's own best interests at heart. Because their own lives in China had been circumscribed by parental and societal constraints that had led invariably to humiliation, pain, and tragedy, the mothers had all come to America to give their daughters a better life, a life of greater choice. Great is the mothers' exasperation, then, when the daughters do not take advantage of the choices available to them or choose unwisely. The daughters realize, too, that their American marriages, with freely chosen mates, have not worked out any better than the arranged marriages of their mothers. An-mei Hsu is puzzled by this:

> I was raised the Chinese way; I was taught to desire nothing, to swallow other people's misery, to eat my own bitterness.
>
> And even though I taught my daughter the opposite, still she came out the same way! Maybe it is because she was born to me and she was born a girl. And I was born to my mother and I was born a girl. All of us are like stairs, one step after another, going up and down, but all going the same way.

An-mei is at first puzzled by and then philosophically resigned to what seems an irrefutable fact that, despite geographical, cultural, and chronological changes, the fate of womankind has not fundamentally changed; it is inevitably tragic.

Achieving Balance in Life

With time, the mothers grow old and weak and give up trying to impose their will on now fully grown daughters. As Waverly Jong puts it, "But in the brief instant that I had peered over the barriers I could finally see what was really there: an old woman, a wok for her armor, a knitting needle for her sword, getting a little crabby as she waited patiently for her daughter to invite her in." Once the daughters are aware of their mothers' vulnerability, their weakness, then all danger is past and the mother may be invited in. The ultimate surrender, of course, is death. But the death of the mother, far from a victory for the daughter, is a tremendous loss.

When An-mei Hsu's grandmother is dying, her mother, long rejected because of a shameful marriage, slices off a piece of her arm for her mother's soup to show the extent that her filial devotion will take her. An-mei Hsu herself bears a scar on her throat emblematic of the years of enforced silence and rejection of her mother, which her uncle and aunt required of her. The dead mother, like the lost motherland, casts a much larger shadow on the living than any of the living mothers and she continues to enforce her will. Jing-mei is initially reluctant to carry out her mother's unfulfilled, long-cherished wish to be reunited with her lost twin daughters, and she complains, "My mother and I never really understood one another. We translated each other's meanings and I seemed to hear less than what was said, while my mother heard more." Her mother, when alive, dismissed with vehemence the suggestion that her daughter resembled her:

> A friend once told me that my mother and I were alike, that we had the same wispy hand gestures, the same girlish laugh and sideways look. When I shyly told my mother this, she seemed insulted and said, "You don't even know little percent of me! How can you be me!" And she's right.

However little the daughter knows about her mother, however ill-prepared and insecure she is, Jing-mei does take her mother's place at the mahjong table and does make the trip to China to see the long-lost twins. And in performing this act of filial obedience, with which the book draws to a close, the daughter realizes that she is not filled with resentment or anger. Instead, in her sisters' faces, to her delight and surprise, she finds her mother.

> And then I see her. Her short hair. Her small body. And that same look on her face. She has the back of her hand pressed hard against her mouth. She is crying as though she had gone through a terrible ordeal and were happy it is over ... And now I see her again, two of her, waving ... As soon as I get beyond the gate, we run toward each other, all three of us embracing, all hesitations and expectations forgotten.

> "Mama, Mama," we all murmur, as if she is among us.

Though Jing-mei may not know her mother any better in death than in life, she, like her twin sisters, carries her mother in her face and in her gestures.... Tan's *Joy Luck Club* ends on a note of resolution and reconciliation. The struggles, the battles, are over, and when the dust settles what was formerly considered a hated bondage is revealed to be a cherished bond.

To be truly mature, to achieve a balance in the between-world condition then, according to . . . Tan . . . one cannot cling solely to the new American ways and reject the old Chinese ways, for that is the way of the child. One must reconcile the two and make one's peace with the old. If the old ways cannot be incorporated into the new life, if they do not "mix" as Lindo Jong put it, then they must nonetheless be respected and preserved in the pictures on one's walls, in the memories in one's head, in the stories that one writes down.

The Joy Luck Club Is Not Strictly Autobiographical

Amy Tan

Amy Tan is the author of The Joy Luck Club, The Kitchen God's Wife, The Hundred Secret Senses, The Bonesetter's Daughter, *and other works.*

When an author achieves fame for writing fiction, many readers assume that the books are at least in some measure autobiographical. Thus, readers tend to confuse events in the novels with actual occurrences in the author's life. Amy Tan does not write autobiography, at least in the way most people think. Her stories may not depict actual events, but they do hold an emotional truth. Specific childhood memories are elusive, more like dreams than actual events, and while Tan does not write stories straight out of childhood memories, she does write with a child's sensibility that allows her to rearrange and reshape experience into fiction.

Sometimes I do get recognized. Most often this happens when I am at the pharmacy to pick up the kind of prescription you would not want to announce at a family barbecue. On one occasion, I was in the waiting room of a medical specialist's office, about to be seen for a routine but loathsome medical procedure.

"Amy Tan?" the receptionist blared. "You're here for a sigmoidoscopy? Did you have your enema yet? Here, take this, and go in that bathroom there.... Say, aren't you Amy Tan, the author? Sure you are! You wrote that movie, *The Happy-Go-Lucky Club*, I saw you in a magazine. Hey, everybody, say hello to Amy Tan."

This, folks, is as good as it gets. Fame and fortune. The American Dream.

The American Dream also comes with a contract to write a memoir. Many people think that this is what I have written in my novels, memoirs disguised as fiction. They tell me, "I don't blame you for divorcing your husband. I divorced mine for the same reason." They ask after my two imaginary children. They tell me they can give me a referral to a top-notch naturopath who cures multiple sclerosis. They ask if I would like to write an article for a chess magazine, since I was, according to my stories, nearly a grand champion.

Now that I've written several memoirs disguised as fiction, some readers assume I may be running out of material. After all, how many times can you write your autobiography? Some of these people offer to give me their stories. They tell me they grew up in a family that was horribly afflicted with tragedy and scandal, disease and death, tears and heartbreak. A few of these strangers have also generously suggested that we split the royalties fifty-fifty. Although it's their story, they concede that I'll be doing most of the writing. They already know who should play them in the film version.

I remember being at a book signing in Houston where a man slipped me a scrap of paper on which he had inscribed what I at first mistook to be a Dadaist poem: "Father hanged, mother murdered, uncle shot, baby son drowned, wife insane, me, almost died twice, all horrible ways. Want to write about me? Call me. Let's talk."

Now, if you were traveling alone in a strange city, would you phone this man and say, "Hey, great ideas, come on over to my hotel so we can get going on them?"

Most of the offers are sincere. I know this. Most people don't even want the fifty-fifty split. They just want me to tell their story, and they need a writer to put the words down in a way others will understand. They want people to know what they have been through. They want witnesses, because it's lonely to go through life with your heartaches. They are people who believe that they can find some sort of redemption, if only their story is told to the world, if only they can get it off their chest.

I feel terrible that I cannot help them. The problem is, I'd never be able to borrow from a stranger's life to create my stories. What's *my* reason for writing the story in the first place, if not to masochistically examine my own life's confusion, my own hopes and unanswered prayers? The metaphors, the sensory truths, the questions must be my own progeny—conceived, nurtured, and fussed over by me.

This is not to say I've been writing autobiographically, at least not in the sense that most people assume. If I write about a little girl who lives in Chinatown and plays chess, this does not mean that I did those same things.

But within that story is an emotional truth. It has to do with a mother who has helped her daughter see the world in a special way. It is a world in which the mother possesses rare magic. She can make the girl see yin when it is yang. The girl sees that her mother, who is her ally, is also her adversary. And that is an emotional memory that I *do* have, this sense of double jeopardy, realizing that my mother could both help me and hurt me, in the best and worst ways possible. So what I draw from is not a photographic memory, but an emotional one. When I place that memory of feeling within a fictive home, it becomes imagination. Anything can happen. The girl may shout back at her mother and tell her to go to hell. The mother may say, "I was wrong. I'm sorry." The possibilities are endless, but one is chosen. And as I write that possibility, it becomes a part of me. It has the power to change my memory of the way things really happened.

For me, writing from memory is more about remembering my psychological place in the world at different stages of my life. Where did I fit in my family, or why didn't I fit. It is about remembering my evolving sense of life, from thinking life was magic, to believing it was random and meaningless, to coming around to thinking it was magic all over again. My memory, then, is entirely subjective. And that, I think, is the kind of memory that is simultaneously the most unreliable *and* the most authentic element a writer can infuse into her work.

For as long as I can remember, I have been curious about how I remember. The earliest memory I have is of an event that took place under a tree. I was a year and a half old. And I know I was that age because of the season and the details of the yard and the house. I remember that I was sitting on the cool lawn on a hot day. Around me was a low fence and to my right was a white house with dark doorways that led to naps. My big brother and parents were above me. Suddenly something hit my head. My brother laughed. Although it did not hurt that much, I was startled and cried loudly to voice my displeasure, lest it happen again. After a while, I picked up what had fallen on my head. It filled my entire palm, a fuzzy golden ball.

"It was a peach," I recalled to my mother.

She thought for a while, and then said that it was not a peach but an apricot, for the parish house in Fresno was the only place we had lived that had a fruit tree in the yard. And this made sense, that it was an apricot, for an apricot would have filled my eighteen-month-old hand in the way a peach would fill my adult one.

There was another time, when I was seven, that I realized that memories were elusive, that you could not will them to stay, and that some you could not will to go away. I was old enough to understand that some things were in my memory like waking morning dreams. No matter how much I tried to hang on to them, they slipped away. And when I tried to find a way to remember them, by, say, writing about them, or drawing a picture of them, the result was not even close. And the result then became the memory that replaced the real thing.

As a child, I tried to develop a number of mnemonic devices. Whenever I felt wronged or misunderstood, I would stare at my hands, the creases in my palms. I would tell myself, I will always be the same person just as I will always have these same hands. I had knowledge that my body would continue to change, although in what ways I did not know precisely. But I stared at my hands and vowed to remember this day, these same hands, and the feeling of injustice I felt in being accused of wrongdoing when it had never been my intention at all.

Looking at my palms today, I can see those splinters from my childhood. I can feel once again the slivers slipping under my skin, hear myself promise never to forget who and what had injured me. I think of those slivers as ingredients for stories. With them, I can concoct thousands of stories, not simply a single bona fide one. The stories I write concern the various beliefs I have held and lost and found at various times of my life. And having now written several books, I realize those beliefs most often have had to do with hope: hope and expectation, hope and disappointment, loss and hope, fate and hope, death and hope, luck and hope. They sprang from the questions I had as a child: How did that happen? What's going to happen? How do I make things happen?

When I write my stories, I do not use childhood memories. I use a child's memory. Through that child's mind, I am too inexperienced to have assumptions. So the world is still full of magic. Anything can happen. All possibilities. I have dreams. I have fantasies.

At will, I can enter that world again.

Social Issues
in Literature

CHAPTER 2

| *The Joy Luck Club*
and Women's Issues

Tan's Young Women Must Rediscover Their Chinese Identity

Walter Shear

Walter Shear has written extensively about American literature. He is the author of The Feeling of Being: Sensibility in Postwar American Fiction.

The eight women's stories in The Joy Luck Club *are a product of the Chinese diaspora (the dispersion, or spreading out of an ethnic group) following World War II that left millions of Chinese separated from their native country and culture. The Joy Luck Club dramatizes this critical transition in cultural values as the older generation of women tries to cling to its roots while the younger generation, immersed in the American feminist revolution, seeks to make a new way in the world. Much of the book's symbolism supports the notion of being lost, as in the key story of "The Moon Lady," where Ying-ying is separated from, and then reunited with her family, but symbolically loses herself. Ultimately, the younger generation of women must reconnect with their Chinese identity in order to heal finally the rupture that began when the older generation left its ancestral home.*

Orville Schell's [19 March 1989] review of *The Joy Luck Club* for the *New York Times* emphasizes that those millions of Chinese who were part of the diaspora of World War II and the fighting that resulted in the triumph of the Communists were subsequently cut off from the mainland and after 1949 left to fend for themselves culturally. Though Schell is

Walter Shear, "Generational Differences and the Diaspora in *The Joy Luck Club*," *Critique*, vol. 34, spring 1993, pp. 193–199. Copyright © 1993 by Helen Dwight Reid Educational Foundation. Reproduced with permission of the Helen Dwight Reid Educational Foundation, published by Heldref Publications, 1319 18th Street, NW, Washington, DC 20036-1802.

struck by the way this book renders the vulnerability of these Chinese women in America, the novel's structure in fact succeeds in manifesting not merely the individual psychic tragedies of those caught up in this history, but the enormous agony of a culture enmeshed in a transforming crisis. What each person's story conveys is the terror of a vulnerable human consciousness torn and rent in a culture's contortions; and although, like other Chinese-American books, this novel articulates "the urge to find a usable past," it is made up of a series of intense encounters in a kind of cultural lost and found. . . .

Generational Differences

In *The Joy Luck Club* Tan organizes her material in terms of a generational contrast by segregating stories of mothers and their daughters. The separate story sections are divided into four parts with mother figures telling two stories, mostly concerned with their past in pre-1949 China, and their daughters telling two stories, one about growing up and one about a current family situation. The exception to this pattern is Jingmei Woo, the daughter of the founder of the Joy Luck Club, who narrates a story in each of the four sections and who adds additional continuity by narrating the first and last section. Though all these people, for the most part, know one another, few of the stories involve contacts with anyone outside the immediate family group. While the daughters' stories usually involve their mothers, the mothers' stories tend to feature a distinct life, involving rather rigid family experiences in old China and their current relationship to their American daughters. By using the perspectives of both mothers and daughters, Tan initially seems to solve what Linda Hunt . . . describes as a basic problem for a Chinese-American woman: "being simultaneously insider (a person who identifies strongly with her cultural group) and outsider (deviant and rebel against that tradition), she cannot figure out from which perspective to speak."

Nevertheless ... the communication barrier here is a double one, that between generations and that created by the waning influence of an older culture and the burgeoning presence of another. Jing-mei announces in the first section: "My mother and I never really understood one another. We translated each other's meanings and I seemed to hear less than what was said, while my mother heard more." Generally, the daughters tend to perceive cultural blanks, the absence of clear and definite answers to the problems of family, whereas the mothers tend to fill in too much, often to provide those kinds of cultural answers and principles that seem to empower them to make strong domestic demands on their daughters....

The mothers tend to depict themselves as, in a broad sense, students learning about the social realities around them and using their experiences to come to conclusions about essential forms of character strength and weakness. For example, one of the mothers, An-mei Hsu, seems to see in her own mother's suicide how to use the world for her own advantage. She not only traces how her mother makes the Chinese cultural beliefs work for her—"suicide is the only way a woman can escape marriage and gain revenge, to come back as a ghost and scatter tea leaves and good fortune"—but also she realizes almost immediately the acute significance of the words of her mother who tells her "she [the mother] would rather kill her own weak spirit so she could give me a stronger one."

Tension Between Mothers and Daughters

Ying-ying St. Clair claims, "I have always known a thing before it happens." Her daughter tends to confirm at least an ironic version of her mother's acquired powers by adding, "She sees only bad things that affect our family." In at least one case the mother's knowledge is a gift passed to the daughter: Waverly Jong opens her story by claiming, "I was six when my mother taught me the art of invisible strength. It was a strategy for winning arguments, respect from others, and eventually, though none of us knew it at the time, chess games." In the last case the knowledge apparently blossoms from the mother's folk saying, "Bite back your tongue," and although Waverly regards it as a secret of her success in chess, she herself is finally a victim of her mother's more authoritarian deployment of the tactic, as it suddenly takes the form of simply ignoring her.

As the last interaction demonstrates, there is nearly always some tension in the exchange between mother and daughter, between old China and the new American environment. Most often the focus is either on a mother, who figures out her world, or on the daughters, who seem caught in a sophisticated cultural trap, knowing possibilities rather than answers, puzzling over the realities that seem to be surrounding them and trying to find their place in what seems an ambivalent world. Strangely, given the common problems presented, there is little concern with peer communication among the daughters. Jing-mei explains, "Even though Lena and I are still friends, we have grown naturally cautious about telling each other too much. Still, what little we say to one another often comes back in another guise. It's the same old game, everybody talking in circles." This difficulty in communication may simply be a consequence of living in what Schell describes as an "upwardly mobile, design-conscious, divorce-prone" world, but it also tends to convey a basic lack of cultural confidence on the part of the daughters and thus a sense of their being thrown back into the families they have grown up in for explanations, validations, and identity reinforcement and definition. . . .

New Culture Versus Old

The Joy Luck Club explores the subtle, perhaps never completely understood, influence of culture on those just beginning to live it. The mother-daughter tensions are both the articulation of the women's movement and the means of specifying the distinctness of Chinese and Chinese-American

A still from the 1994 film adaptation of The Joy Luck Club *shows the main characters posed in mother/daughter groups. From left to right, actresses Kieu Chin, Ming-Na Wen, Tamlyn Tomita, Tsai Chin, France Nuyen, Lauren Tom, Lisa Lu, and Rosalind Chao.* The Kobal Collection.

culture. . . . Behind the overt culture is an odd intuition of a ghost presence, at times a sense of madness waiting at the edge of existence. It is an unseen terror that runs through both the distinct social spectrum experienced by the mothers in China and the lack of such social definition in the daughters' lives. In this context the Joy Luck Club itself is the determination to hope in the face of constantly altering social situations and continually shifting rules. The club is formed during the Japanese invasion of China, created by Jing-mei's mother as a deliberate defiance of the darkness of current events. With a mixture of desperation and frivolity, she and a group of friends meet, eat, laugh, tell stories, and play mah jong. She reasons, "we could hope to be lucky. That hope was our only joy." "It's not that we had no heart or eyes for pain. We were all afraid. We all had our miseries. But to despair was to wish back for something already lost. Or to prolong what was already unbearable."

It is the old China experience that manifests most definitely the enormous weight of fate in the lives of the characters. On the one hand, the constrictive burden is due to the position of women in that society. An-mei seems to regard the woman's role as an inescapable fate: "I was raised the Chinese way; I was taught to desire nothing, to swallow other people's misery, to eat my own bitterness. And even though I taught my daughter the opposite, still she came out the same way. . . . she was born a girl. And I was born to my mother and I was born a girl. All of us are like stairs, one step after another, going up and down, but all going the same way." Another mother, Lindo Jong, is the victim of a marriage arranged when she was only a child. In her struggle to extricate herself from the situation, she does not blame her family who made such arrangements but the society, the town where she grew up, a place she claims is frozen in custom at a time when the rest of China was beginning to change. Although the old culture places the family at its heart, as the experience of the women in this revolutionary situation demonstrates, its attitude toward women begins in the more fluid modern world to tear away at this fundamental unit, making the difficulty of mother-daughter bonding a crucial problem for the culture as a whole.

Ying-ying and the Moon Lady

Ying-ying St. Clair blames herself more than her circumstances, but it is her early social circumstances that structure the experience that so haunts her and cripples her psychically. Situated higher in the social scale of old China than the other members of the club, she seems to fall as a child into a subconscious state from which she never fully recovers, a state that in the social context may stand as a paradigm for individual nightmare in a fragmenting culture. Hers is an episode with a fantasy/folk flavor and a motif of dreaming, which seems to represent a naive, open but mechanical relationship to culture—opposed to a vital reciprocity of being. Ying-ying (the childhood nickname here may be intended to suggest the regressive nature of her trauma) describes her adventures on a boat cruise during the Moon festival, which in her account becomes a symbolic episode, a psychological drifting from the fundamental reality of family. While everyone else sleeps, the little Ying-ying watches in fascination as some boys use a bird with a metal ring around its neck to catch fish. The bird serves its purpose, catching the fish but being unable to swallow them, its social function thus symbolically dependent on an intensely personal, intensely perverse individual frustration.

Finally the boys leave, but Ying-ying stays, "as if caught in a good dream," to watch "a sullen woman" clean fish and cut off the heads of chickens and turtles. As she begins to come back to self-consciousness, she notices that her fine party clothes are covered with the mess of these deaths—"spots of blood, flecks of fish scales, bits of feather and mud." In the strangeness of her panic, she tries to cover the spots by painting her clothes with the turtle's blood. When her Amah appears, the servant is angry and strips off her clothes, using words that the child has never heard but from which she catches the sense of evil and, significantly, the threat of rejection by her mother. Left in her underwear, Ying-ying is alone at the boat's edge, suddenly looking at the moon, wanting to tell the Moon Lady her "secret wish." At this key moment in her young life, she falls into the water and is about to be drowned when miraculously she finds herself in a net with a heap of squirming fish. The fishing people who have saved her are of a class known to her, but a group from which she has previously been shielded. After some initial insensitive jokes about catching her, they attempt to restore her to her family group by hailing a floating pavilion to tell those aboard they have found the lost child. Instead of the family appearing to reclaim her, Ying-ying sees only strangers and a little girl who shouts, "That's not me. . . . I'm here. I didn't fall in the water."

A Loss of Self

What seems a bizarre, comically irrelevant mistake is the most revealing and shocking moment of the story, for it is as if her conscious self has suddenly appeared to deny her, to cast her permanently adrift in a life among strangers. To some degree this acute psychic sense of and fear of being abandoned by their family is a basic reality for all the mothers in this book, each of whose stories involve a fundamental separation from family, an ultimate wedge of circumstances between mother and child.

Though Ying-ying is finally restored to her family, the shock of separation has become too intense a reality. She tries to explain, "even though I was found—later that night after Amah, Baba, Uncle, and the others shouted for me along the waterway—I never believed my family found the same girl." Her self-accusations at the beginning of this story become a miniature autobiography: "For all these years I kept my mouth closed so selfish desires would not fall out. And because I re- mained quiet for so long now my daughter does not hear me. . . . I kept my true nature hidden. . . ." Later she accuses herself of becoming a ghost: "I willingly gave up my *chi*, the spirit that caused me so much pain." She fears that this aban- donment of self has in some way been passed on to her daugh- ter.

"Now," she announces to herself, "I must tell my daughter everything. That she is the daughter of a ghost. She has no *chi*. This is my *greatest shame*. How can I leave this world without leaving her my spirit?" Her first narrative ends with her trapped in the legendary world of old China, still a child but with all the terrible insight into her later life: "I also re- member what I asked the Moon Lady so long ago. I wished to be found."

The *chi* that she refers to may be impossible to render wholly into English, but it involves a fundamental self-respect, a desire to excel, a willingness to stand up for one's self and one's family, to demonstrate something to others. It may well be a quality that the daughters in the book lack, or that they possess in insufficient amounts. Veronica Wang states, "In the traditional Chinese society, women were expected to behave silently with submission but act heroically with strength. They were both sub-women and superwomen." Possibly those cultural expectations, although almost totally erased in American culture, could still survive in residual roles when validated by a concept such as *chi*. . . .

Resolving Cultural Differences

Curiously, in two instances, the generational tensions appear to have their origins in what seems a very American ambition. Waverly feels that her mother leeches off her chess achievements with an appropriating pride, and Jing-mei feels her mother, inspired by a competition with Waverly's mother as well as the belief that in America you could be anything you wanted, pushes her beyond her abilities, at least beyond her desires. The familiar cry "You want me to be someone that I'm not!" accelerates to "I wish I wasn't your daughter. I wish you weren't my mother." and finally to "I wish I'd never been born! . . . I wish I were dead! Like them." The "them" are the other daughters her mother had been forced to abandon in China. This story of Jing-mei moves toward the kind of muted conclusion typical of most of the daughter stories: "unlike my mother, I did not believe I could be anything I wanted to be, I could only be me." There is the sense that this "me" lacks some vital centering, the cultural force that would provide its *chi*.

In the context of cultural analysis, the happiness of the conclusion seems only partially earned by what has preceded it. And the fact that the return and the reunion with the two half-sisters reflect almost exactly the author's own experience suggests that there may be more than a little biographical intrusion here. Ultimately, however, the book's final cultural argument seems to be that there is always a possibility for the isolated "me" to return home. At one time Jing-mei notes, "in a crowd of Caucasians, two Chinese people are already like family." As she makes the return trip to China in the last story, she feels she is at last becoming Chinese. What she discovers in her reunion with her Chinese half-sisters, in her father's story of her mother's separation from these children and from the mother's first husband, and in the photograph of her and her sisters is a renewed sense of her dead mother. The mother's living presence in them is the feeling Jing-mei has been searching for, the feeling of belonging in her family and of being at last in the larger family of China. In this case the feeling of cultural wholeness grows out of and seems dependent on a sense of family togetherness, but the return to the mainland certainly suggests a larger symbolic possibility, one, however, that must still cope with the actual barriers of geography, politics, and cultural distinctness.

Amy Tan [is] empowered by current feminist ideas in [her] examinations of the Chinese-American woman's dilemma. In . . . *The Joy Luck Club*, much of the focus springs out of the mother-daughter relationships and the way the diaspora has created a total contrast in the experiences of mother and daughter. . . .

[*The Joy Luck Club*] testif[ies] to a rupture in the historical Chinese family unit as a result of the diaspora, but seem[s] to believe in a cultural healing. As her conclusion suggests, Tan seems to place . . . emphasis on the Chinese identity as the healing factor.

June's Symbolic Journey to Discover Her Ethnic Identity

Zenobia Mistri

Zenobia Mistri has taught at Purdue University, Calumet. She has written articles on Leslie Marmon Silko's Beet Queen *and Jhumpa Lahiri's* The Interpreter of Maladies.

June Woo's story serves as a central focus for the tales of all the mothers and daughters who cannot understand one another in The Joy Luck Club. *June, as well as the other daughters in the novel, all view the older generation's beliefs as being old-fashioned and Chinese. June Woo's quest to China is symbolic of her inner journey to rediscover her own identity and genealogical ties. It is fitting that she is the only daughter with both an American name (June) and a Chinese name (Jing-mei), for she is the symbolic bond between the old culture and the new. The trip to China is the way in which she reclaims her name and her ethnic background that the older generation holds so dear. The reuniting of three daughters at the conclusion symbolizes that her mother still lives in the faces and bones of her children.*

Amy Tan's short story sequence, *The Joy Luck Club*, focuses on four Chinese mothers and their American daughters who are at odds with their mothers, their inheritance, and the power of their mothers' wisdom and strength. Interestingly, none of these mothers longs for her daughter to be Chinese following nothing but Chinese ways, for each woman has come to America with the intent of making a better life in which her family would know the fabled American successes. Each mother has her own powerful story of overcoming odds, of having learned the lesson of becoming strong through see-

Zenobia Mistri, "Discovering the Ethnic Name and the Genealogical Tie in Amy Tan's *The Joy Luck Club*," *Studies in Short Fiction*, vol. 35, summer, 1998, pp. 251–257.

ing her own mother suffer or by suffering herself. Each mother feels the anguish of the cultural separation between herself and her daughter. Each mother wants her daughter to know the power and advantage of joining the strengths of two cultures instead of embracing only one—the American; and importantly, each mother rescues her daughter from the specific danger that threatens her.

Spatial Structure as Metaphor

The structure of this short story sequence becomes a central metaphor for the thematic elements that link these stories to each other, involving an implicit conversation among the four mothers and their daughters as they tell their stories. The sequence is divided into four sections, each having four stories. Although the stories are about four mothers and their four daughters, only three mothers and four daughters tell their stories in these sections, for June Woo takes her dead mother's place in the first and last sections of the book. She alone has a story in each of the four sections, thus forming the central axis of the book; the first and last sections contain the mothers' stories. The second and third sections are given to the four daughters. Although we read the work sequentially, we continually look back. . . .

The Joy Luck Club works spatially rather than chronologically. We discover pieces of the mothers' childhoods in China as we read their individual stories; we see the breach in the daughters' relationships with their mothers as we read their stories. We understand the repeated symbols, which expand with each use as the stories hold hands at crucial junctures. The theme rounds out with each mother's pain as it expands with each daughter's fear of disappointing her mother. We understand that the cultural divide causes these walls. Each story fits a space on the map that develops for us as we begin to observe the developing and continually shifting picture.

The thematic design for the book evolves through the central story of June Woo and her finding of her ethnic self through her mother. The supporting stories of the other three daughters stand as leitmotifs [themes or patterns] of the fractured relationships between the mothers and their daughters. None of these American-born daughters listens, understands, or respects the power, strength, and wisdom of her Chinese mother. Each of them sees her mother's behavior as if from another continent and is ashamed of her "strange" ways; each daughter fails to understand her mother's need to see American successes coupled with Chinese wisdom and secrets. As the daughters' stories coalesce, showing the lack of understanding, so the mothers' stories fuse showing their pain and feelings of loss—not at their daughters' inability but at their unwillingness to see the power of combining both American and Chinese heritage.

The first and last stories stand as structural and thematic bookends in this collection, and June Woo holds the answer to the puzzle of the 16 stories. Undoubtedly, these stories speak to issues dealing with a bicultural heritage. William Boelhower constructs an approach that cuts across several disciplines such as cultural geography, anthropology, semiotics [the study of symbols], cartography [mapmaking], and the cultural history. This critical approach makes spaces for those elements that we cannot place using traditional literary methods. In accessing the intricacies and nuances in ethnic literature, Boelhower asks [French writer] Jean de Crèvecoeur's question, "Who is the American, this new Man?" Since de Crèvecoeur's time [the eighteenth century], the makeup of the American is very different. In answering the question, Boelhower suggests that to understand the American, one must understand ethnicity and ethnic project or undertaking, in which memory is the crucial factor. Boelhower explains, "Through the processing system of Memory and Project, the subject puts himself in touch with the foundational world of his ancestors, reproduces himself as a member of an ethnic community, and is able to produce ethnic discourse." His analysis suggests germane possibilities for reading and understanding in a more intricate fashion than traditional analysis would permit.

The variety of textual strategies that Boelhower suggests revolve around issues dealing with discovering the self implicit in the surname, the ethnic sign, and memory versus the written word:

> The very ability of the protagonist to stand between the dominant and the ethnic cultures and between the American present and the foundational past of the immigrant generation without losing his ancient soul suggests how time and space are redefined. . . .

This ability is apparent in each of the mothers in *Joy Luck Club*.

June Woo's Spiritual Journey

The opening story places June Woo in the uneasy situation of having to take her mother's place at the Joy Luck Club meeting; later, she is put in the precarious position of having to go to China to fulfill her dead mother's lifelong quest—of being reunited with her long-lost twin daughters. This journey becomes the spiritual, thematic, and structural design of the collection as June Woo discovers her own bonds with her mother and with her ethnic self. Boelhower explains ethnic semiotics: ". . . in the beginning was the name. . . . By discovering the self implicit in the surname, one reproduces an ethnic seeing and understands himself as a social, an ethnic subject. . . . To speak of ethnicity is to speak of ancestry. . . ." June Woo discovers her mother and her ethnic self as she embarks on her journey to China to meet her recently discovered half-sisters. June's reluctance to go to China reflects on the tenuous relationship with her mother. "My mother and I had never really understood one another. We translated each other's meanings and I seemed to hear less than what was said, while my mother heard more."

The trip to China becomes the way in which June Woo claims her name, and the other part of herself, Jing-mei Woo, that she has never understood or accepted. June Woo sets about rediscovering or reconstructing her American ethnic self. Significantly, she is the only daughter with both a Chinese and an American name. She sets the genealogical pattern of understanding her mother and so the ethnic self as she makes this journey to China to be reunited with her twin half-sisters whom she had long assumed to be dead. Boelhower explains how the reconstruction is achieved: "... the subject produces ethnic semiosis (signs) through a strategic use of memory which is nothing other than the topological [concerning the nature of space] and genealogical interrogation of the originating culture of his immigrant ancestors." Memory floods June as she recalls the stories her mother told, in Chinese, of the inception of the Joy Luck Club in Kweilin. She recalls the retelling over the years: "Over the years she told me the same story, except for the ending, which grew darker, casting long shadows over her life, and eventually in mine." Here we see the use of memory to reconstruct the moment in time when the twins were lost. At one level, June's project is the trip to tell the twins that Suyuan Woo is dead; at a deeper level, the trip becomes the journey into the being of her immigrant mother. Like so many immigrant parents, Suyuan Woo has wanted her daughter to be a fantastic American Chinese success. Instead, she has dropped out of college a number of times, changed majors, and is far from the traditionally accomplished immigrant. June Woo feels her own failure and misreads her mother's encouragement as disappointment. In a sense this lack of communication is reflected in the lives of the other three mothers and daughters. Auntie An-mei expresses the imperative for the trip. "But most important, you must tell them about her life. The mother they did not know they must now know." June's reply is the reply of the other daughters. "What will I say? What can I tell them about my mother? I don't know anything. She was my mother."

Mothers Are Alive in Their Daughters

Auntie An-mei speaks to the genealogical tie in powerful ways: "Not know your own mother? . . . How can you say? Your mother is in your bones!" As all the aunts chime in, coaching her on what she should tell about their mother, the nightmare shared by these Chinese mothers becomes clear to June:

> They are frightened. In me they see their own daughters, just as ignorant, just as unmindful of all the truths and hopes they have brought to America. They see daughters who grow impatient when their mothers talk in Chinese, who think they are stupid when they explain things in fractured English. They see that joy and luck do not mean the same thing to their daughters, that to these closed American born minds 'joy-luck' is not a word, it does not exist. They see daughters who will bear grandchildren born without any connecting hope passed from generation to generation.

This passage illustrates the pain of being put aside as being inferior; it articulates the anguish of the forgotten and obliterated, of not having progeny who would look back at ancestral ties with the past. All the mothers, Suyuan Woo, An-mei Hsu, Lindo Jong, Ying-ying St. Clair, fear this genealogical obliteration. June recalls her mother's gift of the jade pendant in "American Translation." She remembers the conversation as a lesson in the blood knot of kinship: "No, Ma,' I protested. 'I can't take this,' 'Nala, Nala'—'Take it, take it'—she said, as if she were scolding me." And then she continued in Chinese. "For a long time I wanted to give you this necklace. See, I wore this on my skin, so when you put it on your skin, then you know my meaning. This is your life's importance."

An-mei Hsu's first story, "Scar," speaks to this blood bond with the mothers before her: "This is how a daughter honors her mother. It is shou so deep it is in your bones. . . . You must peel off your skin, and that of your mother, and her mother before her. Until there is nothing. No scar, no skin, no flesh." Lindo Jong fears her granddaughter will forget her heritage in "The Red Candle":

> It's too late to change you, but I'm telling you because I worry about your baby. I worry that someday she will say. 'Thank you, grandmother, for the gold bracelet. I'll never forget you.' But later she will forget she had a grandmother.

Ying-ying St. Clair also feels the loss of closeness and the separation:

> I think this to myself even though I love my daughter. She and I have shared the same body. There is a part of her mind, which is my mine. But when she was born, she sprang away from me like a slippery fish and has been swimming away ever since. All her life, I have watched her from another shore.

These fears on the part of the mothers are the fears that the genealogical chain that links up with the foundational world of the ancestors will be broken. All the mothers have their memories of the past. Boelhower explains: ". . . it is not a question here of the ethnic subject living in the past but as Sowell says of the past living in him."

These matrilineal [maternal line of descent] fears compound in the book until the last section, where each mother reaches out and forcibly links up with her daughter, showing her the strength she needs to take from her mother and her mother's mother before her. Like women warriors, each mother takes up the challenge and meets it head on. Even timid Ying-ying St. Clair comes forth like the tiger between the trees to rescue her lost daughter. This metaphor of being part of the life substance of their daughters appears in each of the mother's stories. . . .

This theme of not understanding the mothers echoes through the daughters' stories. But it is June Woo who goes to the marrow of the issue in the last story of this cycle. She feels her bones ache with a familiar pain when the train leaves the Hong Kong border and enters China. She recalls her mother's words: "Once you are born Chinese, you cannot help but feel and think Chinese.... It is in your blood waiting to be let go." Now on the train she dreams and imagines. Boelhower explains that without imagination there can be project. He theorizes significant ethnic experiences in ethnic fiction as being generated from a cultural encyclopedia: "When the parents die, their cultural inheritance is passed on to the children; only now they must practice a politics of memory in order to piece together the original patrimony."

Reclaiming the Past

June imagines her sisters' letter to their mother and slowly recovers her Chinese past through pieces of her father's stories coupled with remembering stories her mother had told her; these enable her to weave her generational story all the way back to China.... Here, June chooses to splice memory with the project at hand, which requires her to go forward.

The journey Jing-mei/June undertakes is organized geographically in the text; she goes from San Francisco to Hong Kong, to Shenshen, China, to Guangzhon to Shanghai. Yet, while it is organized geographically, there is a parallel journey being reconstructed for Jing-mei through her mother's and father's stories and recollections. This geographical journey undertaken by her parents in 1949 is recalled and brought back to her as she goes to China for the first time. Both stories—her parents' in the past, and hers in the present—serve to underscore and trace her mother's flight from Kweilin to Chungking, to Shanghai, to Canton, to Hong Kong, to Haiphong, and finally to San Francisco. As Boelhower might explain this: "here the goal is to interpret the past, not the past itself."

The central "project" in *The Joy Luck Club* is Jing-mei's visit to her sisters. Implicit in her name lies the family story and her genealogical link. The pure essence (Jing) coupled with younger sister (mei) mingles. Symbolically, the three of them when united represent the essence of their mother, she who now lives in the faces and bones of her three daughters. They, in turn, signal the coming together of the other three mothers and their daughters. None of their "projects" could have been undertaken without the use of the ethnic encyclopedia—memory, stories, and the imagination. By the end of the journey, Jing-mei Woo understands the past as she understands what her mother means to her, as do the other daughters. The "Queen Mother of the Western Skies," the last story in the sequence, reflects on "The Joy Luck Club," the first story in which June Woo sits at her mother's place, facing East. The Western part of June Woo understands the Eastern inheritance of Jing-mei Woo as she asks her father to tell the missing part of her mother's Kweilin story. He starts in halting English, and she asks him to tell it in Chinese. Jing-mei Woo has arrived.

Damaged by Their Mothers' High Expectations

Wendy Ho

*Wendy Ho has taught in the Asian American Studies depart-
ment at the University of California, Davis. She has also served
as the director of the Asian Pacific American Cultural Politics
Research group.*

The mothers in The Joy Luck Club *have all suffered their share
of misfortune and loss before coming to the United States. All
four try to teach their daughters how to understand life and react appropriately to various situations. Because they themselves
have been devalued in American society as women who speak
only broken English, they push their daughters to succeed and
even to excel. When their daughters cannot or will not rise to
the levels their mothers envision, the mothers become frustrated
and take out their disappointment on their daughters. Each
mother and daughter pair experiences a love-hate relationship,
and the younger women rebel, escape, or sabotage their own success.*

The Joy Luck mothers fiercely nurture and socialize their
young daughters into womanhood through the 1950s and
into the 1980s. What becomes clear is that all the mothers—
whether they directly or indirectly tell their daughters their
good intentions—want to protect them from the oppressive
circumstances that they and their foremothers endured in
China in their personal and social lives. They want their Chinese American daughters to have the best life—not to dupli-
cate the sad, tragic, or restricted lives they and their mothers

have known. "In America I will have a daughter just like me. But over there nobody will say her worth is measured by the loudness of her husband's belch. Over there nobody will look down on her, because I will make her speak only perfect American English. And over there she will always be too full to swallow any sorrow! She will know my meaning, because I will give her this swan—a creature that became more than what was hoped for." Tan's mothers want to teach their daughters how to read situations clearly and how to stand up and fight for themselves; hard lessons learned in their lives. They want daughters who will be bolder, more self-assured women; who are independent from their husbands; who will have good jobs, status, and voice; who feel their own merit.

High Expectations for Daughters

Furthermore, as ambitious but devalued working-class immigrant mothers who speak "broken English," they put their energies into realizing or translating the "daughter/woman of their desires" in a conservative, mainstream middle-class American context as well. That is, they attempt to turn out college educated, yuppie daughters who can acculturate and assimilate into mainstream American society—who can speak perfect English, get a good job, maintain a comfortable, financially secure lifestyle, fit in as they themselves could not. In this effort, they have been successful. Their daughters do achieve a level of economic success and social mobility that their mothers did not have as immigrant women.

Joy Luck mothers all seem to hold on tenaciously to visions of something better, even as they live their lives in compromised and negotiated circumstances as daughters, mothers, and wives in China and later, in the United States. Some of the mothers possess (or think they possess) the sheer power to will their perfect daughters into existence by whatever means. These mothers have *nengkan*—a can-do spirit that seems to steamroll beyond fate, beyond circumstances, beyond daughter. They nurture and educate children, hold their families together, cook, clean, and, if need be, do paid work in and out of the home. Such mothers are willing to sacrifice material goods, family, and a personal life for their daughters to succeed. Suyuan Woo cleans people's houses daily to supplement her husband's income in order to pay for "extras" like piano lessons for her daughter. She dreams up schemes for a perfect daughter. She has a notion of her daughter as a child prodigy, a genius who would excel in her new circumstances in America. Suyuan, An-mei, Lindo and Ying-ying believe their daughters, regardless of their actual abilities, could do and be anything they set their mind to. "You can be best anything."

Furthermore, some of the Joy Luck mothers zealously pressure their daughters to be hard workers and achievers; rules and discipline are signs that they deeply care about their daughters' survival and happiness. Affection is not often displayed in an effusive "touchy-feely" manner; rather, it is dispensed in disciplinary, tough-love doses. The mothers think they have lovingly and ambitiously mapped out their daughters' lives for their own good—even though this may not be the way their Americanized daughters see the game plan. What becomes obvious is the high cost of such survival and love. Emotional bullying can become a form of fierce and frightening love between mothers and daughters.

Reflections of Their Mothers

In part, each daughter becomes a reflection of her mother as she could be anew, a self enacting viable options in new circumstances. The Joy Luck mothers hold up the mirror and see themselves perfected in their daughters, especially as they perceive and dictate perfection. With the birth of her baby girl Waverly, Lindo Jong becomes dissatisfied with the shortcomings in her own life—the years of socialization into submission in her mother-in-law's household and the suppression of her private self. She wants her daughter to turn into a beautiful swan—a perfect, happy, and independent woman. Each mother desires her daughter to demonstrate visibly that she is the most obedient, most respectful, beautiful, and talented swan-daughter. Such a daughter becomes the mother's status symbol or trophy of her success in the United States, achieved after great suffering and disappointment in her own life. In the eyes of a Joy Luck mother, only such a daughter will ameliorate the social and emotional pain of leaving China, mother, and family for life as an outsider in American culture. This is a massive investment and transference of love and ambition that can take a serious toll on mother-daughter relationships.

In return for their maternal work, Tan portrays the longings of the Joy Luck mothers to be loved, understood, obeyed, respected, and memorialized by their daughters. The mothers do not wish to be forgotten. Many maintain few or no links with their families in China; their daughters become the intimate link to past and future: Who will memorialize them and their histories if not their own daughters and granddaughters? The great fear among the mothers is that their daughters do not really know them and do not respect them, their work, advice, or stories. It is with much ambivalence and trepidation then that they look to their daughters to keep their stories and preserve their cultural heritage. What they had hoped for was a daughter with a Chinese mind/character like theirs but in new circumstances—a rather difficult positioning for American-bred Chinese daughters to negotiate gracefully or seamlessly.

Frustrated by Failure

Tan's stories continually demonstrate how Joy Luck mothers are frustrated by their daughters' failures. Despite the mothers' efforts to preempt stumbling or errors, their Chinese American daughters fall into traps (often similar to their mothers') in their relationships with each other, with their families and with men. The mothers think their daughters do not know how to select true friends and allies. In part, the mothers blame their daughters' dismal circumstances on their failure to believe or listen carefully to their mothers. In addition, the daughters have no *nengkan* (an ability to accomplish anything one puts their mind to) like their mothers; they have no *shou* (respect) for, or *chuming* (inside knowing) of their mothers. The daughters lack the backbone, self-esteem, perseverance, loyalty, and responsibility to get on with their lives. At times, their daughters seem tired, isolated, and lost, uncertain about what next to do or how to extricate themselves from dead-end relationships and situations. Even when lost, these grown women still have a hard time returning to their mothers for love and advice. The mothers stand by wondering what happened to all their efforts to realize an American version of the ideal Chinese daughter.

The reactions of the Joy Luck mothers to their frustration and anger over these stupid, disobedient, imperfect daughters can be withering. An-mei Hsu wonders whether the cycle of women's oppression can ever be broken: "And even though I taught my daughter the opposite, still she came out the same way! Maybe it is because she was born to me and she was born a girl. And I was born to my mother and I was born a girl. All of us are like stairs, one step after another, going up and down, but all going the same way." Waverly Jong is a chess champion, nurtured by her mother's support and advice. However when Lindo Jong realizes her daughter's ingratitude for all her efforts, she feels insulted and attacks furiously. Lindo ominously threatens her daughter, "We not concerning this girl. This girl not have concerning for us." As a result, Waverly Jong has a crippling nightmare about a chessboard and an all-powerful chess queen mother as opponent who wears a triumphant smile and has eyes like "two angry black slits." Mother Lindo reclaims her ascendancy by checkmating her daughter's presumption to the title of consummate chess queen and strategist. Similarly, for all her best-

A game of mah jong. This traditional Chinese game is prominently featured in The Joy Luck Club. David Allan Brandt/Riser/Getty Images.

intentioned efforts to improve her daughter's prospects, Suyuan Woo also thinks her daughter Jing-mei is spiting her efforts. She draws the line when she tells Jing-mei that there are only two kinds of daughters: "Those who are obedient and those who follow their own mind! Only one kind of daughter can live in this house. Obedient daughter!" In the view of the mothers, only such a daughter can be trained as a woman warrior and ally—according to her mother's rules and desires, of course.

The Joy Luck mothers think that they can transform their ugly-duckling daughters into swans without the daughters having memory of being a goose or duck, that is, without living their lives and making mistakes, without the painful process that the mothers themselves went through. Some mothers try to protect their daughters by force-feeding them the lessons and strategies they have derived from their own bittersweet lives. In this process, these Chinese mothers expect their daughters' strict and unquestioning attention and obedience.

Sometimes in their ambitious designs for their daughters, the mothers fail to consider carefully their daughters' dilemmas and what their needs and hopes might be as second-generation Chinese women in America.

A Love-Hate Relationship

Just as mothers love and hate their daughters, so do their daughters love and hate them. The loving dedication to Tan's *The Joy Luck Club* states: "To my mother and the memory of her mother. You asked me once what I would remember. This and much more." And yet, Tan as a rebellious daughter painfully confesses to a time when she "hated [her] life. Wished [her] mother was not [her] mother." On the one hand, mothers can be viewed as nurturing, loving, and protective of their daughters. Suyuan Woo tells her daughter Jing-mei what she wants for her: "Only ask you be your best. For your sake. You think I want you be genius? Hnnh! What for! Who ask you!" On the other hand, a mother can also be perceived as hateful, self-centered, excessively controlling and frightening. The mother's love, ambitions and expectations for her daughter are not always experienced by the daughter in kindly, grateful ways. The definitions and perceptions of mothers and daughters about their roles and responsibilities as women cause a great deal of the miscommunication. . . .

Tan continually portrays this emotional tug-of-war in the daughters between the love and hate, between the awe and the fear they feel for their mothers as they seek to gain a degree of autonomy for themselves. For instance, in the face of rejection by Waverly, Lindo Jong ignores her much adored but ungrateful daughter. She no longer advises or hovers over Waverly; she neither polishes her trophies nor cuts out newspaper articles featuring her daughter. Waverly is worried; mother is silent. It seems that her mother had "erected an invisible wall and [she] was secretly groping each day to see how high and how wide it was." Waverly begins to lose at chess tournaments and feels she has lost her earlier "magic armor" and "supreme confidence" in her chess skills. She translates these circumstances as her mother's way of destroying her with secret strategies and tricky side attacks to her weakest points.

Rose Hsu Jordan also senses the possible consequences of attempting to go against her mother. In her dream, Rose picks a doll entirely different from the one that her mother knew she would pick. "Stop her! Stop her! cried her mother [An-mei Hsu]. As I [Rose] tried to run away, Old Mr. Chou chased me, shouting, 'See what happens when you don't listen to your mother!' And I became paralyzed, too scared to move in any direction." The perceived withdrawal of a mother's awesome love, nurture, and inner knowing—*chuming*—of her daughter, is a frightening prospect for a daughter even though she may simultaneously wish to escape or rebel against mother herself. The daughters find it extremely difficult to escape someone who has protected them since childhood. No one seems to know or love them so intimately as their mothers— who were once daughters, too.

Dangerous Rebellion

Indeed, as Tan demonstrates, there is real psychic danger in a daughter's drive to escape from her mother's control. Jing-mei Woo's story demonstrates how self-destructive a daughter's rejection of her mother can be. In her youth, Jing-mei Woo is very resentful of her mother's ambitious prodding. Suyuan thinks her daughter could be a Chinese version of Shirley Temple, Peter Pan, or a classical pianist. These American models of perfection and success grow as Suyuan culls through stories about amazing—not ordinary—children from *Ripley's Believe It or Not, Good Housekeeping,* and *Reader's Digest.* There are nightly tests to see what Jing-mei excels at, and the nightly disappointments written like a text on her mother's face as she continually fails the tests. For a while Jing-mei herself is filled with a grandiose sense of herself as a prodigy, of a soon to be perfect daughter, the apple of her adoring and adored mother's eyes. She imagines herself in Western storylines and images—Cinderella, Christ child, a ballerina. To be ordinary for mother or like mother is just not enough.

But her mother's ambitions and expectations are so overwhelming at times that she feels crippled in her ability to think or act on her own behalf. The additional outcome of these pressures is the nagging fear in Jing-mei that she will be nothing. She begins to feel inadequate in her inability to meet her mother's high expectations, expectations often rooted in the mainstream cultural models of American society her mother has appropriated to fulfill her dreams for a better life in America. Jing-mei's feeling of failure grows through her life: she gets no As, is a mediocre pianist and becomes a college dropout. All her life she is frustrated by "raised hopes and failed expectations." She begins to blame her mother for many of her problems in life.

To counteract the power of her mother, she becomes a rebel, a saboteur of her mother's plans. Jing-mei discovers the rebellious side of herself. In a mirror she sees a reflection of her ordinary face as powerful, stubborn, angry. "I had never seen that face before. I looked at my reflection, blinking so I could see more clearly. The girl staring back at me was angry, powerful. This girl and I were the same. I had new thoughts, willful thoughts, or rather thoughts filled with lots of won'ts. I won't let her change me, I promised myself. I won't be what I'm not." She sets up a defensive oppositional stance to her mother; she aggressively *reacts* rather than acts, which does violence to their potential bonding. Both mother and daughter stop honest communication. They withdraw in cold, distant silence:

> And for all those years, we never talked about the disaster at the recital or my terrible accusations afterwards at the piano bench. All that remained unchecked, like a betrayal that was

now unspeakable. So I never found a way to ask her why she had hoped for something so large that failure was inevitable.

And even worse, I never asked her what frightened me the most: Why had she given up hope?

It is only in her thirties that Jing-mei realizes that in sabotaging and silencing her frustrated mother, she has sabotaged herself, too. In "Best Quality," she makes some painful realizations after her mother's death: she is a small time copywriter; she can't outsmart Waverly; and she can't choose a good crab: "That was the night, in the kitchen, that I realized I was no better than who I was." After all these years of trying to be special and resenting her mother for it, what she begins to feel is "tired and foolish, as if I had been running to escape someone chasing me, only to look behind and discover there was no one there." Like Waverly, Rose, and Lena, she has been so busy fighting off her own overblown image of a powerful, suffocating mother that she has neglected to search into her own inadequacies and motivations. This extreme reaction by a daughter to her mother gets in the way of her ability to love her mother and act on the best choices in her own life.

Storytelling Reconciles Mothers and Daughters

Gloria Shen

Gloria Shen has taught at the University of Georgia. She has published articles on comparative poetics, narrative techniques, society and literature, and problems in women's literature.

The Joy Luck Club uses sixteen separate stories to explore the relationship between four mother-daughter pairings. These interlocking stories depict relationships that are uniquely Asian American and, at the same time, universal. Because the demanding mothers and their increasingly independent daughters experience a significant generation gap, the mothers must use biographical stories to share their past, connect with their daughters, and help them to understand the forces that have caused the mothers to become the people they are. These stories have the effect of strengthening mother-daughter bonds and allowing the daughters to become mature individuals who appreciate their mothers' ways.

In *The Joy Luck Club*, [Amy] Tan probes the problematic mother-daughter relationship in sixteen separate stories spanning two generations of eight women. Though the eight characters are divided into four families, the book itself is concerned more with an unmistakable bifurcation along generational lines: mothers, whose stories all took place in China, and daughters, whose stories deal with their lives in America. Though the mothers all have different names and individual stories, they seem interchangeable in that they all have similar personalities—strong, determined, and endowed with mysterious power—and that they all show similar concerns about

Gloria Shen, *International Women's Writing: New Landscapes of Identity*. Westport, CT: Greenwood Press, 1995. Reproduced by permission of Greenwood Publishing Group, Inc., Westport, CT.

their daughters' welfare. As a result, the mothers are posses- sively trying to hold onto their daughters, and the daughters are battling to get away from their mothers. The four mothers and four daughters are different, but their differences remain insignificant as the action of the novel is focused on the per- sistent tensions and powerful bonds between them.

Tan's characters are seen in both detail and outline. The first-person testimonies allow the reader to examine each of the characters closely and to develop a sense of empathy with each of them; but, at the same time, the testimonies reveal a pattern, particularly in the way the mothers and daughters re- late to one another. The purpose of this treatment is obvious: to portray the mother and daughter relationship as both typi- cal and universal.

In Tan's novel, The Joy Luck Club is a bridge uniting both space and time. The Joy Luck Club connects the sixteen intri- cately interlocking stories and helps to reveal and explain the infinite range and complexity of mother-daughter relation- ships. Within the narrative, it joins two continents and unites the experiences of the mothers and the daughters. The Ameri- can daughters are alien to Chinese culture as much as they are to their mother's uncanny, Chinese ways of thinking. To the daughters, cultural and ethnic identity is possible only when they can fully identify themselves with their mothers through their maturation into womanhood. The sharing of cultural experiences between mothers and daughters through the de- vice of storytelling transforms structurally isolated mono- logues into meaningful dialogues between mother and mother, daughter and daughter, and, more important, mother and daughter and coalesces the sixteen monologues into a coher- ent whole. While the mother and daughter relationships are unique in the ethnic context of Tan's novel, they also have a universal aspect. Indeed, all women share this experience, re- gardless of time and space. An-mei Hsu is puzzled by both the specific and universal qualities of the mother-daughter relationship. Raised traditionally, she was taught to swallow her desires, her bitterness, and the misery of others. Rejecting her upbringing, she tries to instill in her daughter a strong sense of self. Unfortunately, her daughter is a passive individual. An-mei Hsu is thus convinced that regardless of their respective upbringing, mothers and daughters are somehow condemned to being similar: "And even though I taught my daughter the opposite, still she came out the same way! Maybe it is because she was born to me and she was born a girl. And I was born to my mother and I was born a girl. All of us are like stairs, one step after another, going up and down, but all going the same way." . . .

Symbols and Images

Tan's extensive use of symbols and images creates a mood of expression that reveals and explains the infinite range and complexity of these mother-daughter relationships. Each of the four sections of *The Joy Luck Club* begins with a prologue, defining the theme of that section while disclosing certain aspects of the problem in the mother-daughter relationship. The first prologue contains a cluster of images that highlight the nature of this relationship in the book and summarize the whole novel. This prologue centers around an old woman who remembers that, while still in Shanghai, she bought a swan for a small sum. The swan, according to the vendor, was once a duck who had managed to stretch his neck in the hope of becoming a goose. On the boat sailing to America, the old woman swore to the swan that she would one day have a daughter whom no one would look down upon, for she would speak only perfect English. In order for this daughter to know her mother's meaning, she would give her the swan.

However, upon arriving in America, the swan is confiscated, and the old woman is left with only one of the swan's feathers. This feather is far too insignificant for her to convince anyone, least of all her daughter, how beautiful the swan was. Furthermore, the daughter she had hoped for has become an unsympathetic "stranger" who does not even speak her language. The prologue thus ends on a poignant note. Indeed, year after year, the mother waits for the moment when she would be able to tell her daughter in perfect American English that the feather is far from worthless, for it symbolizes all of her "good intentions."

The prologue sets the tone and the reasons for the tensions and conflicts in the mother-daughter relationship. The "swan" and the "old woman" who sailed across the ocean together, "stretching their necks toward America," are an emblem of the four mothers who came to the United States, hoping to give their daughters a better life than the one they had in China. The "good intentions" are clearly stated. But the mother, left with an almost worthless feather, is condemned to wait patiently many years until the daughter is finally mature enough to come back to her, to appreciate her, and to reconstruct the beautiful swan from the feather. The swan is therefore emblematic of both the mother's new life in America and, more important, her past one in China, an experience the mother wants to communicate to her daughter. However, only a mature daughter, who has overcome the psychological and cultural gap separating her from her mother is capable of coming to terms with this experience.

The Central Issue Is Mothers and Daughters

The mother-daughter relationship is the central issue and focal point in the dialogues between the mothers and daughters in Tan's book. The novel traces the psychological development of the American daughter and her final acceptance of the Chinese mother and what the Chinese mother stands for. Jingmei Woo, who replaces her recently deceased mother at the mahjong table, is the first to tell a story on behalf of her mother; she is also the very last daughter to recount her own story. It is interesting to note that when she is asked by her three "aunts" to go to China in order to fulfill her mother's long-cherished wish to meet her lost twin babies, Jing-mei shocks and upsets them with her confused yet honest remark that she would not know what to tell her sisters because she did not really know her mother: "What will I say? What can I tell them about my mother?"

The mothers are all frightened by this response. Indeed, they sense in it the confusion of their own daughters. In Jing-mei, they recognize their own daughters, all as ignorant and as unmindful of the truths and hopes their mothers brought over with them from China. Ironically, the accomplishment of the mother's dream for her daughter, a dream that entailed her physical removal from the motherland, results in multifarious problems in the relationship with her daughter.

In Tan's novel, the Chinese mothers are all strong-willed, persistent, hard to please, and overly critical. They often make their presence and their goodwill look like outrageous impositions rather than tacit influences. When, for example, Jing-mei Woo describes her mother's New Year crab dinner, we learn that, although she does not like this dish, she is obliged to eat it since her refusal to do so would constitute a rejection of her mother's love. The food and the advice offered by the mothers are hard to refuse not only because they are a symbol of love but also because they tend to carry the full weight of maternal authority. That is why Waverly Jong is convinced that telling one's mother to be quiet would be tantamount to committing suicide. In another example, Waverly tries to make her mother accept her American boyfriend by showing her a fur coat that he has given her as a token of his love. Totally dejected by her mother's antagonism toward her boyfriend, whom the mother does not consider good enough for her daughter, Waverly Jong feels distressed at not being able to shake off her mother's clutching influence. When she looks once again at the coat her mother has just finished criticizing, she becomes convinced that it is, indeed, shabby. . . .

A Lack of Communication

The alienation between mother and daughter often stems either from a lack of understanding or from various forms of miscommunication. While the daughters, all born in America, entirely adapt to the customs and language of the new land, the immigrant mothers still hold onto those of China. All the mothers feel their daughters' impatience when they speak Chinese and are convinced that their daughters think they are stupid when they attempt to communicate with them in broken English. If Jing-mei is initially reluctant to carry out her mother's long-cherished wish to be reunited with her two lost sisters, it is mainly because she believes that she and her mother have never understood one another. The language barrier that existed between them was such that both mother and daughter imperfectly translated each other's words and meanings.

In a tragicomic incident that exemplifies the futile attempt to bridge the mother-daughter gap, Lindo Jong is proudly speaking to her daughter about Taiyuan, her birthplace. Waverly mistakes Taiyuan for Taiwan and is subsequently visibly irritated when her mother loudly corrects her. The daughter's unintentional mistake, combined with the mother's anger, destroys their attempt to communicate. Consequently, they are both plunged, once again, into a steely silence. In another example of Tan's lightness of touch straining with ambivalence, Lena St. Clair defines her mother as a "displaced person" who has difficulties expressing herself in English. Born in Wushi, near Shanghai, she speaks Mandarin and only a little English. Lena's father, who spoke only a few canned Chinese expressions, always insisted that his wife learn English. Unable to express herself clearly in English, she communicates through gestures and looks and sometimes in a broken English punctuated by hesitations and frustration. Her husband thus feels justified in putting words in her mouth.

The mothers' inability to speak perfect American English has multiple ramifications. For one thing, as they themselves have not lived in a foreign country, the daughters are left with the false impression that their mothers are not intelligent. As a result, the daughters often feel justified in believing that their mothers have nothing worthwhile to say. Furthermore, when mother and daughter share neither the same realm of experience and knowledge nor the same concerns, their differences are not marked by a slip of the tongue or the lack of linguistic adroitness or even by a generational gap, but rather by a deep geographical and cultural cleft. When the mother talks about American ways, the daughter is willing to listen; when the mother shows her Chinese ways, the daughter ignores her. The mother is thus unable to teach her daughter the Chinese ways of obeying parents, of listening to the mother's mind, of hiding her thoughts, of knowing her own worth without becoming vain, and, most important of understanding why "Chinese thinking is best." . . .

A Ferocious Struggle

The daughters' battles for autonomy and independence from powerful imposing mothers are relentless, and the confrontations between mothers and daughters are fierce. In the chapter "Without Wood," daughter Rose Hsu Jordan describes the decision she made as a child in her dream to pick a different doll from the one her mother expected her to choose. Another daughter, Jing-mei, adopts a self-defensive strategy against her mother's expectation that she be a child prodigy by disappointing her whenever she can. She does this by getting average grades, by not becoming class president, by not being accepted into Stanford University, and finally by dropping out of college. By consistently failing her mother, Jing-mei manages to assert her own will.

The struggle between mother and daughter is equally ferocious. It often takes the form of psychological warfare between the two. Waverly Jong, a child prodigy chess player, envisages this struggle as a chess game in which her mother is transformed into a fierce opponent whose eyes are reduced to "two angry black slits." The struggle is also expressed in physical and verbal fights. When, for example, the daughter Lena St. Clair overhears a mother and daughter who live next door shouting and fighting, she is not overly surprised when she learns from the daughter that both of them "do this kind of stuff all the time."

The Device of Storytelling

In spite of the daughters' successful resistance and rejection of their influence, the mothers valiantly refuse to give up. After having tried many different strategies throughout their lives, the mothers finally discover that storytelling is the best way to reach the hearts and minds of their daughters. Realizing that sharing her past with her daughter might be the last and only trump card she has in order to "save" her daughter, Ying-ying St. Clair decides to give it a try. Her decision, nevertheless, reflects her awareness of the nature of the clash—the daughter's lack of ethnic and cultural identity, which Ying-ying is convinced will lead to her daughter's unhappiness. By telling her past to a daughter who has spent all of her life trying to slip away from her, Ying-ying St. Clair hopes to reclaim her, "to penetrate her skin and pull her to where she can be saved."

Jing-mei Woo's dying mother also realizes that her daughter's problem similarly stems from her refusal to embrace her Chinese roots. Indeed, before her trip to China, Jing-mei relentlessly denies her Chinese heritage. On the train to China from Hong Kong, Jing-mei finally comes to terms with her true identity. Reflecting on her past, she admits to feeling different. Furthermore, she is now prepared to concede: "[M]y mother was right. I am becoming Chinese."

The device of storytelling by women to women is employed extensively throughout the novel as a means to achieve various ends. For instance, it is the means by which Lindo Jong is physically set free. As a young girl, Lindo managed to get out of an arranged marriage. She accomplished this feat by inventing stories about her husband's ancestor's wish for him to marry a servant girl. The mothers also resort to storytelling when trying to impart daily truths and knowledge to the daughters. Through storytelling, they hope to help their daughters rise above negative circumstances or simply avoid unknown dangers. . . .

Reconciliation Through Storytelling

Through the sharing of personal experiences, a reconciliation between mothers and daughters is reached. The daughters realize that their mothers have always had their best interests at heart. Echoing the old woman and the swan in the first prologue at the beginning of the novel, mother Lindo Jong explains her feelings most poignantly: "I wanted everything for you to be better. I wanted you to have the best circumstances, the best character. I didn't want you to regret anything." Because their own lives in China had been circumscribed by social and parental constraints that invariably led to pain, humiliation, and tragedy, the mothers all came to America to give their daughters a better life. However, daughters must first understand the real circumstances surrounding their mothers: how they arrived in their new country, how they married, how hard they tried to hold onto their Chinese roots. Once they have understood this, the daughters are better able to understand why they themselves are the way they are. Ultimately, this understanding will also lead them to finally appreciate their mothers. The mothers try very hard to leave an imprint of themselves on their daughters through various means. For the mother Lindo Jong, names carry a symbolic significance. She tells her daughter that the reason she named her Waverly is that, when she gave birth to her, they lived on a street with the same name. In naming her thus, she was convinced that her daughter would feel that she belonged on that street and that when it would come time for her to leave home, she would take with her a "piece" of her mother. While Waverly is left with a "piece" of her mother in her name, An-mei Hsu inherits from her mother a ring of watery blue sapphire, and Jing-mei receives a necklace with a jade pendant from hers. These pieces of jewelry are also symbolic of their mothers' continued presence in their lives. However, the daughters' acceptance of, and identification with, their mothers does not take place until all of them come into contact with their mothers' past through stories. Thus, after her mother's death, when she sets foot on Chinese land for the first time in her life, Jing-mei learns about her mother's long-cherished wish. Also during this trip, she discovers the meaning of her mother's name as well as the meaning of her own name: her mother's, Suyuan, means "Long-cherished Wish," and hers, Jing-mei, means "Younger Sister of Pure Essence." After learning the hidden meanings of these names, Jing-mei is full of remorse: "I think about this. My mother's long-cherished wish. Me, the younger sister who was supposed to be the essence of the others. I feed myself with the old grief, wondering how disappointed my mother must have been."

The sharing of cultural experience between mother and daughter through the device of storytelling transforms the naive, self-protective daughters, who try hard to move away from, or surpass, their ethnic roots, into the mature daughters who are appreciative of their mother's Chinese ways. Through storytelling, the daughters come to accept their mothers' and their own race and are willing to seek their ethnic and cultural roots.

The Maternal Line of Descent Dominates *The Joy Luck Club*

Helena Grice

Helena Grice has taught at the University of Wales, Aberystwyth. She is the author of Beginning Ethnic American Literatures *and* Maxine Hong Kingston.

Like other women's Asian American novels, The Joy Luck Club *revolves not around a patriarchal society, but a matriarchal one. Thus matrilineage, or the maternal line of descent in a family, is a major theme in the book. From the early symbolism of Jing-mei's invitation to take her dead mother's place at the mah-jong table through the other women's stories, matrilineage figures prominently. The younger women are so dominated by their mother that they believe the older women possess magical powers. Nevertheless, they all actively rebel, each in her own way, until the novel resolves itself by reasserting the mother-daughter bonds and the maternal line of descent.*

Amy Tan's first novel *The Joy Luck Club* tells the story of four women (Suyuan, An-mei, Lindo and Ying-Ying) who were born in China, and who later emigrated to the United States. All four women have American-born daughters (Jing-mei, Rose, Waverly and Lena), and it is the intergenerational relationships between these eight women which preoccupies Tan's novel. . . . [I]t has been phenomenally successful. Starting with advance dustjacket praise from Alice Walker and Louise Erdrich, amongst others, it stayed for nine months on the *New York Times* bestseller list, was reprinted in hardback twenty-seven times, selling more than a quarter of a million copies in hardback alone. . . . [I]t was also a finalist for the

National Book Critics Circle Award, as well as the National Book Award. As Penny Perrick wryly observed in 1991, 'Whether by a quirk of literary fate or because it is their psychological destiny, Chinese American women seem to have won the world rights to the mother-daughter relationship'. Clearly, [Chinese American author] Maxine Hong Kingston to some extent paved the way for Tan's success, in so far as her own work [*The Woman Warrior*] popularised the themes of female friendship and filiality, and in this sense at least, both texts appear to be fashioned from the same cloth. Yet, as Sauling Wong points out in a perspicacious essay on Tan, entitled 'Sugar Sisterhood: Situating the Amy Tan Phenomenon', Tan's text has been marketed quite differently from Kingston's:

> Like Maxine Hong Kingston's *The Woman Warrior* (1976), *The Joy Luck Club* is a crossover hit by a female ethnic writer; it also straddles the worlds of 'mass' literature and 'respectable' literature, stocking the shelves of airport newsstands as well as university bookstores, generating coffee table discussions as well as conference papers.

Wong suggests that the key to Tan's success lies in the convergence of a specific Asian American matrilineal tradition (which she delineates in some detail), and a white feminist ideological need for matrilineal literature, a need which is also bound up in orientalist discourse. Wong suggests that Tan herself colludes in the purveyance of an exotic China to a white readership, and this is very reminiscent of early reactions to Kingston's writing. We should remember that Kingston, too, was fiercely attacked for her perceived exoticisation of Chinese American culture twenty years earlier. Aside from these similarities, one very noticeable difference between the two texts is an element Wong gestures towards in the quotation above: Tan's novel is something of a lowbrow cultural version of Kingston's. Whereas Kingston's preoccupation with the mother-daughter dyad [twosome] is but part of an extensive meditation upon intercultural and intra-cultural understanding, Tan's concern with mothers and daughters is the predominant focus. Similarly, despite its tight structure, Tan's novel lacks the formal complexity and elegance of *The Woman Warrior*, with its palimpsestic [layered] narration, polyvocality, and shifting cultural registers. . . .

Maternal Line of Descent

[A] matrilineage [maternal line of descent in a family] is constructed . . . explicitly in *The Joy Luck Club*. Mother-daughter relations are both emphasised and foregrounded. Each section of the text itself begins with a mythical Chinese parable about the relations between mothers and daughters. Structurally, the organising framework of the text, the separate narratives of four mothers and four daughters, is explicitly concerned with the construction of a matrilineage, and all of the sections are either narratives of separation from, or connection to, the mother. Daughter Jing-Mei Woo's story opens the text and it immediately sets the theme of matrilineage: her mother Suyuan Woo has died, and Jing-Mei has been asked by the other mothers to take her place at the weekly mah-jong game. Mah-jong is a Chinese game played with dice and tiles, in which four corners, or winds, compete. The mah-jong game structurally acts as a trope [metaphor] in the novel for the matrilineage—it is both a connection between the mothers, but also the daughters. In this opening section, the matrilineal connection is seen to be both symbolically and actually threatened, through the collapse of the mah-jong game. The other mah-jong players want Jing-Mei to go to China to learn about and reconnect with her maternal history by meeting her mother's first children. Jing-Mei's unease at this proposition represents her ambivalence towards matrilineality and this in turn threatens the psychological link between her and her mother. Because Jing-Mei's story is the framing narrative in the text the pattern is thus set of both a yearning towards, and a resistance to the matrilineage. Like *The Woman Warrior*, the matrilineage in *The Joy Luck Club* works through 'talking story', with the mothers reciting tales of their lives to their daughters.

Following Jing-Mei's section are the three narratives of the mothers, Lindo, An-Mei and Ying-Ying. These sections are preoccupied with the threatened disruption of the matrilineal connection, initiated by Jing-Mei's paradigmatic rejection of her maternal history. All the mothers go on to tell stories of the separation from and/or loss of their own mothers: An-Mei's of her own mother's banishment from the family home; Lindo of how she was given to another family in marriage and Ying-Ying of the separation from her mother at the festival of the Moon Lady. Lindo expresses their collective anxiety when she says of her daughter: 'I worry that . . . she will forget'. The mothers' mournings of the loss of their own mothers strengthens the growing sense of the disappearance of the matrilineage. Ying-Ying says of her own daughter: 'we are lost, she and I, unseen and not seeing, unheard and not hearing, unknown by others'. Even though the loss is actually of the connection between mothers and daughters, the mother's inability to break free from her daughter here is expressed in her continuing identification with her: although her daughter has elected to move away from the mother, the mother sees this as a tragedy for *both*.

The Magical Powers of Mothers

The mothers' narratives of feared or actual loss or separation within the mother-daughter dyad are balanced by the following narratives of their daughters. It is significant within the symbolic construction of the text that Tan has the daughters follow the mothers, which could be seen as a hint of resolution. These daughterly stories articulate four concerns specifically related to the matrilineage. All of the daughters pay homage to the power of their mothers. . . . Both Rose and Lena also believe that their mothers have magical powers. The mothers are celebrated as all-knowing, as Lena says, 'to this day, I believe my mother has the mysterious ability to see things before they happen'. Often, this power is passed on to the daughter: 'my mother taught me the art of invisible strength'. However, in the world of mother-daughter relations this recognition of strength cannot be read as a simple celebratory gesture, as some critics do. The daughters recognise that whilst maternal power can be passed on to the daughters, it can as easily be used against them. For instance, daughter Waverly Jong's reluctance to tell her mother about her husband-to-be stems from the knowledge of her mother's power, as she notes: 'my mother knows how to hit a nerve'. Similarly, the nightmares that another daughter, Rose Hsu Jordan, suffers from as a child stem from her mother's power over her. She says of her mother 'The power of her words was ... strong'. Through instances like these, we can see that Tan's attitude towards mothering in the novel is complex, perhaps even contradictory. She seems to veer between a celebratory impulse, which does nothing to demystify mothering as an activity, and a far more negative version in which the all-powerful and all-knowing mothers become suffocating and damaging influences upon their daughters. The mothers know the daughters better than anyone else and are repeatedly shown as looking beyond their daughters' representations of their behaviour. Lena's mother tells her husband that she does not like ice cream, for example, and Jing-Mei's mother knew that her daughter would pick the inferior crab at a feast, because she would have done that herself.

Despite the recognition of closeness and similarities, the Joy Luck daughters struggle against their mothers and the imposition of a matrilineage. Jing-Mei actively tries to reject the mother-daughter bond: 'I wish I wasn't your daughter' she tells Suyuan, as Waverly does too when her own mother demands: 'embarrass you be my daughter?' The struggle is enacted in an attempt to escape the stifling and repressing impo-

Refugees fleeing Communist forces crowd Soochow Creek in Shanghai, China, December 21, 1948. The mothers in The Joy Luck Club *all came to America to escape the decades of warfare that ravaged China and led to a Communist takeover in 1949.* AP Images.

sition that the mother's influence is perceived to be. Partly this is a result of the mother's situation as mediator of the Chinese mother-culture, a cultural inheritance the daughters are not sure that they want. Because matrilineality cuts across cultural lines in the novel, the acceptance of the connection to the mother is also an acceptance of this cultural inheritance, further problematising an already complex relationship.

Reconnecting with the Mother

Towards the end of the novel, the daughters ultimately initiate attempts to reinstate the matrilineal connection, and this provides the forward thrust of the plot. It is Lena's dream of a daughter saving her mother that symbolically enacts this move. Then, after her mother's death, Jing-Mei starts to play the piano, an act that would have pleased her mother. Rose takes the advice from her mother that she has previously rejected and Waverly visits her mother and tells of their shared genealogy. These initial actions all begin to signal the affirmation and acceptance of the matrilineage on the part of the daughters. This acceptance is both a recognition of the inter-subjective connection between mother and daughter, and an acceptance of the mother culture. This move is then extended by the following three mothers' narratives, which affirm the reinstated matrilineage through a series of stories the mothers tell about the cultural history and genealogy they share with their offspring. An-Mei relates the tale of the reconciliation and reunion she experienced with her own mother years earlier. Ying-Ying talks about both the physical closeness she shares with her daughter: 'she and I shared the same body', as well as the inter-subjective engagement between them: 'there is a part of her mind that is a part of mine', before seeking to strengthen the connection between them by storytelling about her past: 'and now I must tell her everything about my own past. It is the only way to penetrate her skin and pull her to where she can be saved'. So, matrilineal healing of the rift between mother and daughter, as in *The Woman Warrior* and [Joy Kogawa's novel] *Obasan*, takes place through storytelling. Thomas Ferraro describes this impulse to 'talk-story' as the Chinese mothers and daughters call it, as a 'possible antidote' to the wounds both mothers and daughters have sustained in these texts, and it certainly seems to become an increasingly urgent and important project in the mothers' eyes. The fourth mother, Lindo, also tries to heal the rift between her and her daughter in an episode at the hairdressers called 'Double Face'. As her own and her daughter's similar faces are reflected in the same hairdresser's mirror ('these two faces, I think, so much the same!'), she remembers a similar occasion with her own mother and notes: 'I am seeing myself and my mother' again enforcing the matrilineal connection. The move towards matrilineage and the recognition of inter-subjective dependency is reflected structurally in the final sections of the novel. For the most part, the novel uses a first-person narrative mode, but in these last sections the narrative voice shifts from first-person address to a more deliberate second-person address: the daughter figure is the specifically intended listener. The section titles: 'Double Face', 'Half and Half' and 'Two Kinds' also reflect the coupling in the mother-daughter dyad. Finally, Jing-Mei's return to China completes the return to maternality. The matrilineage is thus confirmed both in east and west: Jing-Mei's visit to China and her meeting with her Chinese sisters also symbolises the acceptance of culture-as-motherhood too.

Mother/Daughter Relationships in the Post Women's Liberation Era

Bonnie Braendlin

Bonnie Braendlin is a feminist critic. She is the author of Authority and Transgression in Literature and Film, *and the editor of* Cultural Power/Cultural Literacy: Selected Papers from the Fourteenth Annual Florida State University Conference on Literature and Film.

Much has changed in literature and life since the women's liberation movement of the 1960s and 1970s. Feminist novels influenced by this movement often suggested that women needed to sever their ties with authority figures such as their mothers or husbands to be fully independent. Liberation could only come through death, rejection of one's children, or divorce. But the subsequent decades have altered perceptions of women's independence, and verbal interactions that do not privilege, or hold superior, one way of thinking over another (as traditional societies often privilege men's or elder's opinions) represent a preferable alternative to radical gestures. In this sense, the ending of The Joy Luck Club *mirrors changing feminist ideology, as the daughter does not have to reject, but instead may incorporate, her mother's legacy.*

In the 1970s I became, almost simultaneously, a feminist teacher/critic and the mother of a daughter. While analyzing novels emerging from the Women's Liberation Movement, where daughters struggle to free themselves from enslaving ideologies of wife/motherhood, I tended to identify with the

Bonnie Braendlin, *From Private Voices, Public Lives: Women Speak on the Literary Life.* Edited by Nancy Owen Nelson. University of North Texas Press, 1995. Copyright © 1996 by the University of North Texas Press. Reproduced by permission.

daughters and to deplore the maternal machinations of fictional mothers, often characterized as little more than co-opted wives in cahoots with domineering fathers to coerce rebellious daughters into traditional wife/mother roles. As a mother of a daughter in an era when feminism was demanding a place for women in male-dominated culture, I often felt the conflicts among my perceived duty to socialize her toward survival and success in a masculine world, my determination not to replicate my own mother, and my desire to be my own woman and to let my daughter be hers. And just as often my daughter seemed caught between her need for parental direction and her desire for independence. . . .

Women Struggling for Independence

Antagonisms between mothers and daughters in U.S. history and literature became particularly acute during and after the 1970s, when the women's movement—advocating equality in a man's world—defined subjectivity in masculinist terms that privileged independence, self-sufficiency, and autonomy at the expense of traditional "feminine" relational values of nurturing and caring. Because these values had been embodied in an ideology of motherhood defined and dominated for years by patriarchal males, daughters of the liberation movement viewed them as outdated restrictions foisted upon them by their retrograde mothers. Defining themselves in ways formerly allowed only to men, "liberated" daughters wanted to usurp the traditional son's position, to move out of the home and into the workplace, to climb the ladder of success. . . .

Conflicts between mothers of one generation and daughters of another are inscribed in numerous text of the liberation era, for instance [in novels such as] Rita Mae Brown's *Rubyfruit Jungle*, Alice Walker's *Meridian*, Lisa Alther's *Kinflicks*, Margaret Atwood's *Lady Oracle*, and Maxine Hong Kingston's *The Woman Warrior*, all published in the early to mid-seventies. In *Kinflicks*, independence for the daughter necessitates both divorce and rejection of her own child, and her mother's abrogation of maternal control. The novel represents maternal self-sacrifice as a fatal blood disease, implying that mothers must die in order for daughters to live. Hong Kingston's fictionalized autobiography also portrays the mother-daughter relationship as antagonistic and obstructive to female development, but she at least spares the mother, and at the end her "Song for a Barbarian Reed Pipe" unites autonomy, nurturing, and artistry, albeit in a fantasy of utopian female solidarity. . . .

In the eras following the women's liberation movement, we daughters of the seventies have become disillusioned with and conscious of our own co-option in masculinist ideologies and our efforts to replicate our fathers at the expense of maternal values; we've begun to identify with the mothers we had formerly rejected, thus complicating what formerly seemed to be a simple daughter versus mother conflict. Women can now, if they wish, be nurturing without being servile and can encourage men to care about others, protect and nourish relationships. In both fictional and critical texts, moreover, we are moving from antagonistic dialectic arguments—which were often (among critics and between mothers and daughters) really monovocal power plays—to more polyvocal, more dialogic, forms of spoken and written communication.

Dialogism Defined

Diagolism, according to [twentieth century Russian critic] Mikhail Bakhtin, is the constant interaction among meanings expressed in spoken or written communication, insuring that no word, ideology, or discourse is privileged [i.e., superior] or remains privileged, even when it is supported by some kind of authority. In life, the development of individual subjectivity (personhood or self) occurs in the context of one's social and cultural languages (discourses); during the development process, when adolescents and young adults are encouraged—or coerced—into internalizing the discourses of their elders, conflicts arise because the new generation also resists becoming the old. But while individuation is the process by which a society indoctrinates its young into its value systems, it also creates a space for defiance of tradition and of choice among other, competing ideologies. Resistance to and re-evaluation of old values, coupled with new choices, introduce new voices into society; thus as the young grow up into adulthood, becoming modified versions of their parents, they promote and insure sociocultural change (if not, necessarily, progress). In the novel, Bakhtin suggests, the interaction among discourses appears as dialogues among characters, between an author and the characters, between readers and texts, and among various ideologies that permeate a work, linking text and contexts. Literary characters may be read as representing various subject positions, beliefs and behavior patterns that shift and change as the characters act and react within their fictional milieu. And we as readers interpret literature in the context of our own lives; who we are—our cultural, social, political, and psychological selves—guides our reading. Those selves, of course, change over time, modifying the way we read.

Living in a Post-Feminist World

As my daughter grows up, I am changing as a mother, becoming less concerned about guiding her development and more willing to appreciate her as a fellow adult, a young woman who struggles to make her own decisions, to become the person she wants to be, while retaining something of her parents' values and mores. She, I can tell, vacillates between resistance to becoming like me and a desire to emulate those qualities in me she admires. And my reading of literature continues to be guided by my own experiences as a daughter/mother and also by my study of contemporary feminist theory. Increasingly, feminist authors, theorists and critics—as we wrestle with issues of gender, race, and class, of history, ideologies, and aesthetics—are calling into question binary oppositions such as culture/nature, male/female, and mother/daughter. Cultural feminist theorists are redefining these putatively "natural" oppositions as socially constructed and thus dependent upon consensus for their continued existence and also open to modifications. Not only have I changed as a reader and critic since the 1970s, but women-authored novels have changed as well, reflecting the increased diversity of American culture and the literary scene, as formerly marginalized and silenced women and ethnic groups voice their perspectives. Published in 1989, Amy· Tan's *The Joy Luck Club* both imitates and revises works like *Kinflicks* and *The Woman Warrior*, which antedate it by some fifteen years. Tan's novel depicts the socialization of young women as a dialogical process in which the mother/daughter opposition becomes more complicated, with mothers and daughters still antagonistic, but also more accepting of the similarities between generations. Instead of one daughter confronting one mother, Tan creates four mothers (three living and one deceased) and four daughters—contemporary young women caught in the marriage/motherhood discourse of western bourgeois capitalism. In conflict with their mothers, who embody marital/maternal ideologies of old China, the daughters express their desire for individuality and independence, often entailing divorces from marriages that entrap them in "other-defined" roles. While their mothers object to these separations and appear to coerce their daughters into remaining in marital "enslavement," their own stories of their early lives in China reveal a female desire for self-definition and resistance that transcends generations, closing generational gaps. And, unlike earlier novels where the daughters' stories predominated, even to the extent of eclipsing the mothers' autobiographies, *The Joy Luck Club* foregrounds the mothers as characters and narrators who tell their own stories. . . .

Resolving Issues Through Dialogism

The mother-daughter dialog(ic)s of Tan's novel inscribe various discourses, both traditional (for example, patriarchal ownership of women, the sacredness of motherhood) and resistant (as in the desire for independence and selfhood). These are not exclusively expressed by either the mothers or the daughters; although communication between the two is hindered by differences in language and social orientation, both mothers and daughters share inherited beliefs about wife/mother roles that empower and disempower women. Both are in conflict over simultaneous desires to comply with and to resist society's demands and definitions of women. And although the mothers feel compelled to persuade their daughters to accept prescribed marital and maternal duties, they too resist total compliance with demands made by these roles. Some readers of *The Joy Luck Club* complain that its ending, with daughters reunited with one another and with the spirit of the dead mother, is too easy, too simplistic, too utopian in light of the continued conflictual relationships between "real" mothers and daughters. As a feminist mother in the nineties, I read the ending of the novel, where Jing-Mei Woo holds her long-lost Chinese sisters in an embrace, as a resurrection and vindication of their dead mother, who longed to reunite her daughters, and as a rewriting of earlier novels where lone daughters repudiated their mothers' desires. Like *Kinflicks*, Tan's novel kills off a mother, but then replicates her in her daughter, creating a matrilinear [maternal line of descent] genealogy of resemblances less utopian than that in *The Woman Warrior*. It can also be argued that closure in Tan's novel applies an Eastern philosophy of "both/and" to a Western predicament of either (daughter)/or (mother).

Female Empowerment in *The Joy Luck Club*

Patricia P. Chu

Patricia P. Chu has taught at George Washington University.

Tan's novel echoes the utopian myth of immigration. In this myth, the immigrant abandons the old world for the promise of the new, and, despite encountering numerous obstacles in the new world, eventually overcomes these difficulties through hard work and perseverance. This myth emphasizes the importance of the immigrant woman's agency, or willpower. The first episode of the novel, a tale in which the immigrant woman buys a goose but is left only with a tail feather to present to her daughter, symbolizes this struggle. The subsequent stories interweave the mother-daughter relationship and the immigrant assimilation plot. June (Jing-mei) becomes truly empowered as the chronicler of all of the women's stories. While authorship is traditionally associated with men and women often need outside authorization for their efforts, June functions as Amy Tan's surrogate in voicing the stories of the other women.

Let's begin, then, by speaking briefly about the relationship between the "mother-daughter romance," as I shall call it, and the utopian myth of the immigrant's Americanization that underlies it, noting that Tan's version shares with the generic myth certain values central to American thinking: the belief in America as a land of opportunity, the bonds between parents and children, and the power of the individual to control his or her own future through acts of will (agency). In the immigration myth, immigrants abandon an old world, which, like the home of a mythic hero, has become incomplete, disordered, or intolerable, to brave the journey to America, which is figured as a promised land of greater economic and social opportunity as well as greater freedom and justice. Although the immigrant may encounter substantial difficulties in America, he or she typically overcomes these difficulties by remaining true to the initial dream of American society's fairness and openness, working hard, and looking forward to the greater success and assimilation of his or her American-born children. This narrative typically emphasizes the power of the immigrant's agency and the ultimate attainability of the American dream and denies that obstacles such as racism or economic exploitation are systemic or insurmountable. This utopian view of American immigration is the foundation of Tan's text.

The Mother-Daughter Narrative and the Immigration Myth

Built directly upon this foundation is the mother-daughter narrative, which affirms the desire of each generation for the respect and understanding of the other, and the importance of maternal legacies of wisdom and character transmitted from mother to daughter. This plot, in which each mother guides her daughter to claim greater agency in her own life, tallies nicely with the immigration plot. Together, the two plots comply with a fictional condition deeply embedded in American popular culture, the premise that heroic individuals can triumph over all obstacles.

The novel opens with a short episode—a prelude to the first four stories—that epitomizes the whole book's skillful blending of the mother-daughter romance and the immigration myth. In the mother-daughter romance, mothers seek their daughters' understanding and offer in turn a legacy of gendered, ethnically marked identity and empowerment. On one level, the text insists that this legacy is transmitted instinctively and genetically—"through the bones," as one character will say—but the text as a whole makes *narrative* the prime medium for transmission of the maternal legacy. The primary function of the prelude, then, is to signal that the stories to follow will fulfill the crucial functions of cultural transmission and translation. This opening story also embodies three components of the maternal narratives that are shortly offered at greater length: first, a narrative in which girls and women are educated to accept social powerlessness as their due, first in long-ago China and then in contemporary America; second, a counter-narrative of female empowerment through individual efforts of will; and third, a narrative of successful immigration and assimilation, processes that provide avenues of escape from the closed system of Chinese society.

The Swan Story

In the story, an old woman remembers a swan she once bought in Shanghai, which, according to the vendor, had transcended its original identity as a duck by stretching its neck in the hope of becoming a goose. Instead, it became something better: a swan "too beautiful to eat." As the woman carries the swan to America—both travelers stretching their necks in aspiration—she fantasizes:

> "In America I will have a daughter just like me. . . . Over there nobody will look down on her, because I will make her speak only perfect American English. And over there she will always be too full to swallow any sorrow! She will know my meaning, because I will give her this swan—a creature that became more than what was hoped for."

> But when she arrived in the new country, the immigration officials pulled the swan away from her, leaving the woman fluttering her arms and with only one swan feather for a memory. And then she had to fill out so many forms she forgot why she had come and what she had left behind.

Now the woman was old. And she had a daughter who grew up speaking only English and swallowing more Coca-Cola than sorrow. For a long time now the woman had wanted to give her daughter the single swan feather and tell her, "This feather may look worthless, but it comes from afar and carries with it all my good intentions." And she waited year after year, for the day she could tell her daughter this in perfect American English.

This Chinese American "ugly duckling" tale captures a number of ideas central both to this text and to other narratives of immigration: the old world as a place of limited possibility; the immigrant as the one duck who will not accept her appointed place in that society; America as the site of the immigrant's dream of transformation, the land of unbounded possibility; the blurring of the immigrant's vision and sense of self when confronted with the realities of an alien and inhospitable land; the transference of hope (the swan feather) to the immigrant's offspring; the dream of vicarious assimilation through those offspring, who will be both like and unlike their parents (fully comprehending the parent yet fully assimilated); and, finally, the fear of alienation from and rejection by the offspring. The daughter's affinity for Coca-Cola and unfamiliarity with sorrow serve as shorthand for issues to be elaborated in the novel: the danger that the material comfort, even luxury, symbolized by the drinking of bubbly, unnourishing Coca-Cola will also lead to malnourished character development, a callousness and lack of imagination bred by the very prosperity, and shelter from suffering, that the mother has risked so much to offer. The story ends with the immigrant mother poised between hope that her daughter may still be brought to understand the world of meaning symbolized by the swan's feather and fear that the moment for transmitting that legacy may never arise.

Your Mother Is in Your Bones

The opening chapter, which follows this passage, emphasizes this interweaving of the mother-daughter and assimilation plots. June Jing-mei Woo, whose mother, Suyuan, has just died, is invited by her mother's friends ("aunties") and her father to take her parent's place at the weekly meeting of the mahjong club her mother founded, the Joy Luck Club. Like bridge, mahjong is a four-handed "card" game (played with engraved tiles rather than cards). June knows she is to play her mother's hand at this meeting, but this turns out to be true on more levels than one. After the game, her father and "aunties" reveal that June's half-sisters, lost in China in their infancy, have at long last been located. Alas, it has happened too late for them to meet their mother, Suyuan. Thus, June is to go to China to greet them in her mother's place, break the news of her death, and bear witness to her life. When June doubts that she knows her mother well enough to perform this task, her aunties erupt in dismay:

> "Not know your own mother?" cries Auntie An-mei with disbelief. "How can you say? Your mother is in your bones!"
>
> "Tell them stories she told you, lessons she taught, what you know about her mind that has become your mind," says Auntie Ying, "your mother very smart lady...."
>
> "Her kindness."
>
> "Her smartness."
>
> "Her dutiful nature to family."
>
> "Her hopes, things that matter to her."
>
> "The excellent dishes she cooked."
>
> And it occurs to me. They are frightened. In me, they see their own daughters, just as ignorant, just as unmindful of

all the truths and hopes they have brought to America. They see daughters who grow impatient when their mothers talk in Chinese, who think they are stupid when they explain things in fractured English. . . . They see daughters who will bear grandchildren born without any connecting hope passed from generation to generation.

Woman as Storyteller

Thus, June, a drifting copywriter who has not yet found her true subject, is officially assigned the task of remembering and representing her mother (both speaking for and portraying her). By implication, she is chosen to be the chronicler for her mother's generation. Clearly, June is Amy Tan's fictional surrogate, for she inherits not only the immigrant offspring's classic call to remembrance but the writer's call to authorship. Male writers, like James Joyce's Stephen Dedalus, are often portrayed as eagerly seizing the hammer and anvil of authorship ("to forge in the smithy of my soul the uncreated conscience of my race" [*Portrait of the Artist*]); by contrast, women writers, especially ethnic women writers, often need the legitimation of outside authorization for their writing. Here Amy Tan offers her alter ego, June, official family cover for taking up the perhaps unwomanly or unfilial task of writing for publication: it is a duty to her mother, family, and community. The link between June and the author is further suggested by this novel's dedication, which addresses the book to Tan's mother and grandmother and offers it as a kind of memory in response to remembered conversations. In short, the charge of *The Joy Luck Club* initiates a roundelay of interlaced first-person stories in which June, as the author's surrogate, imagines the voices and stories of the mothers and daughters. Only Suyuan, being dead, does not voice her own first-person narrative; instead, June takes her two turns in the narrative as well as the mahjong game.

Tan's Beginning Rejects Stereotypes About Immigrant Women

Catherine Romagnolo

Catherine Romagnolo has taught at Trinity College in Washington, DC.

The Joy Luck Club's opening myth about coming to America has been criticized as being false and nonreflective of true Chinese values. However, Tan was not trying to construct a traditional cultural tale but instead to undermine and oppose stereotypical notions about immigrant women in America. Rather than telling a simple success tale, Tan's book is more complex, and many of the women's stories reject the original goals of gaining selfhood and discovering one's identity. Their stories reflect a repudiation of the traditional notion of a woman's identity as fixed and static. Instead, despite acknowledging the importance of the past, their stories reject the notion that one's history is completely knowable and focus on the women as agents of their own identity formation.

The *Joy Luck Club* begins with what has been described by Asian American writer and cultural critic Frank Chin as a "fake" myth of origin:

> Then the woman and the swan sailed across an ocean many thousands of li wide, stretching their necks toward America. On her journey she cooed to the swan: "In America I will have a daughter just like me. But over there nobody will say her worth is measured by the loudness of her husband's belch. Over there nobody will look down on her, because I

Catherine Romagnolo, "Narrative Beginnings in Amy Tan's *The Joy Luck Club*: A Feminist Study," *Studies in the Novel*, vol. XXXV, spring 2003, pp. 89–107. Copyright © 2003 by the University of North Texas. Reproduced by permission.

will make her speak only perfect American English. And over there she will always be too full to swallow any sorrow! She will know my meaning, because I will give her this swan—a creature that became more than what was hoped for."

This "fake Chinese fairy tale" is so described both because, according to Chin, it overstates the misogyny of Chinese society, and because it represents a misappropriation, a "faking," of Chinese culture. The implication of this misappropriation, Chin argues, is that Chinese Americans—particularly women—like Tan and her characters are so assimilated that they have lost touch with their "Chinese" cultural origins. Consequently, they have produced new feminized "versions of these traditional stories," which in trying to pass themselves off as authentic only represent a further "contribution to the stereotype," a stereotype which facilitates the emasculation of Asian American men.

Not Fake, but Fabricated

We may take this myth to exemplify the structural opening, that is, the beginning lines/pages of Tan's novel. While other theories of narrative beginnings might identify this section of the text as the beginning, its purpose is not as self-evident as might be suggested. . . . In fact, while the structural opening of *The Joy Luck Club* may initially appear to be trying (and failing, according to Chin) to establish and mythologize an authentic and originary moment of immigration from China to U.S.A. for the "Joy Luck aunties," it, in fact, disrupts the very notion of authenticity, especially in regards to origins. Although the first half of the myth seems to imply an unproblematic transition between Chinese and American cultures, by its ending, the contradiction between an idealized version of assimilation to "American" subjectivity and the fragmentation of identity that historically marks immigrant experiences becomes clear: "But when she arrived in the new country, the immigration officials pulled her swan away from her, leaving the woman fluttering her arms and with only one swan feather for a memory. And then she had to fill out so many forms she forgot why she had come and what she had left behind." Instead of either idealizing an essential Asian origin or mythologizing a melting-pot ideology of U.S. immigration, Tan's structural narrative opening marks the way "America" strips the woman of her past, her idealized hopes for the future in the United States, and excludes her from an "American" national identity: the woman is still waiting "for the day she could tell her daughter this [narrative] in perfect American English." By opening with a fabricated myth of origin, Tan's novel foregrounds the ideological implications of a search for beginnings and exemplifies the importance of narrative beginnings to an understanding of this text.

Undermining Cultural Stereotypes

As Chin's response attests, Tan invokes a mythic sensibility in these opening lines, yet undermines the authority of nationalist myths of origin that attempt to uncover an uncorrupted past ethnic identity. . . . Through an ironic use of mythic form, language, and tone, Tan utilizes repetition for subversion. Repetition in this sense is a performance, which has "innovation," to use [critic] Trinh Minh-Ha's term, as its goal. Trinh explains:

> Recirculating a limited number of propositions and rehashing stereotypes to criticize stereotyping can . . . constitute a powerful practice . . . Repitition as a practice and a strategy differs from incognizant repetition in that it bears with it the seeds of transformation . . . When repitition reflects on itself as repitition, it constitutes this doubling back movement through which language . . . looks at itself exerting power and, therefore, creates for itself possibilities to repeatedly thwart its own power, inflating it only to deflate it better.

Tan's opening myth utilizes mythic characters such as "The old woman" juxtaposed with historically rooted figures like immigration officials. It invokes mythic situations seemingly ungrounded in time such as a journey across an ocean "many thousands of li wide" contrasted by modern cultural icons like Coca Cola. Her myth, then, reflects upon itself as national mythology, revised. In its self-reflexivity and difference, this formal and generic repetition serves to deflate the power of the so-called original. That is, by mimicking supposedly authentic nationalist mythologies, the self-consciously illegitimate status of Tan's myth exposes the inability of any nationalist project to recover a genuinely original, pure cultural history.... Because culture is always hybrid, any project that asserts purity must necessarily be "fake." This "fakeness" should not, however, be read as inauthenticity, but as a deconstruction [undermining] of the very concept of authenticity.

The self-conscious repetition and revision of Tan's myth simultaneously destabilizes the notion of an authentic cultural origin (which gives rise to essentialist conceptions of gendered and racialized identities) and dislodges stereotypical representations of Chinese culture. For although the language of this structural opening might evoke a mythological aura, in its content Tan's opening myth reflects the hybridity of immigrant subjectivity. That is [according to social critic Lisa Lowe], it signifies the historical "relationships of unequal power and domination" that accompany Chinese immigration to the United States. Moreover, it combines and interrogates stereotypically "Chinese" cultural symbols like the swan and "American" cultural emblems like Coca Cola: "Now the woman was old. And she had a daughter who grew up speaking only English and swallowing more Coca Cola than sorrow." In such cases, Tan utilizes overdetermined cultural symbols, which most readers would recognize as the trite, even clichéd, images that have come to signify the respective cultures. And yet, because of the way in which they are deployed, the repetition of these stereotypes cannot take hold as authentic representations; their authority is subverted. The symbol of the swan, stereotypically representative of Chinese women as graceful, silent, and docile, is hybridized and re-appropriated within Tan's narrative. It comes to symbolize both the woman's past ("the old woman remembered a swan she had bought many years ago in Shanghai for a foolish sum") and her idealized hopes for the future as an American ("I will give her this swan—a creature that became more than what was hoped for"). In combining these contradictory impulses or desires (nativism and assimilation), the symbol becomes unstable, unfixed, never to be resolved within Tan's revisionist myth. Furthermore, as this symbol (the swan) is torn away from the old woman when she reaches the United States, we apprehend both the historical violence of immigration as well as the illusory nature of nativist and assimilationist mythology: "She forgot why she had come and what she had left behind."

There Is No Authentic Immigrant Experience

Tan also invokes a stereotypical emblem of Americanness in the materialistic and modern cultural icon, Coca Cola. Yet, like the symbol of the swan, this sign is already unstable and dislocated from its supposed referent. For, while Coca Cola has come to represent "Americanness," in fact, in this period of late-capitalism the corporation of Coca Cola is found throughout the world. The transnational character of this icon registers the economic and cultural imperialism entailed in the success of Americanization on a global scale, while contradicting its status as American; for, it both is and is not American. This instability continuously interrogates what it means to be "American." That is, the Coca Cola icon does not have as its referent some real originary "America," but alludes to a popular representation of Americanness as tied especially to diversity ("I'd like to buy the world a Coke") [a popular Coca-

A protestor at the inauguration of President Richard Nixon in 1969 calls for women's rights. David Fenton/Hulton Archive/Getty Images.

Cola jingle]. This image is not only a cultural myth unto itself; it also points back to other media representations of America, which refer back yet again to the popular representation of America in "melting pot" ideology, a construction which has historically contributed to the elision of a United States that is, in reality, fraught with racial contradictions. Thus, through the chain of signifiers set in motion by the Coca Cola icon, Tan's myth not only subverts the authority of cultural symbols, but confirms cultural identity to be discursively constructed. Finally, through the placement of these icons in an opening narrative which undermines its own status as a myth of origin, *The Joy Luck Club* structurally reaffirms the inadequacy of such "authentic" cultural symbols to represent the "original essence" of their cultures. The final effect of this myth, then, is not a reconciliation of contradictions—assimilation and nativism—but a dialogic representation of an immigrant experience that struggles with both of these impulses.

By positioning an obviously spurious myth at the structural opening of *The Joy Luck Club*, Tan gives her own text a false originary moment and thus further critiques the notion of origins. The duplicity of this opening structurally and symbolically undermines the text's status as an "immigration novel" that could somehow refer to and represent the "authentic" female immigrant experience. That is, by placing a false myth of origin—which refers only to other illusory origins—in the inaugural pages of her text, Tan implies metaphorically that the novel can never be said to recover any sort of authentic, definitive experience. . . .

Quests That Reject Their Goals

Tan's structural opening is additionally significant in that it acts as a synecdoche [a part of a larger whole] for the thematic concerns of the novel. Through its preoccupation with a search for authenticity, origin, and/or the defining moment of one's identity, the story helps us to recognize links between structure and thematic origins. This thematic interest in beginnings is placed in dialogue with the text's structural openings, reinforcing its cultural critique. For example, Suyuan Woo, who has already died as the novel opens, has spent her entire life in an unsuccessful quest to recover the fateful moment when she left her babies on the roadside in Kweilin while fleeing from the invasion of Japanese soldiers. Symbolically, she tells her daughter Jing Mei (June): "The East is where things begin . . . the direction from which the sun rises, where the wind comes from." An-Mei Hsu is also preoccupied with a quest. Her narrative tells the story of an attempt to recover the source of her psychic pain as well as a search for a mother who was absent for much of her childhood. She speaks of this past as a wound: "That is the way it is with a wound. The wound begins to close in on itself, to protect what is hurting so much. And once it is closed, you no longer see what is underneath, what started the pain." And Ying Ying St.

Clair, who is similarly in search of a lost self, remembers the sense of loss that accompanied her youth: "The farther we glided, the bigger the world became. And I now felt I was lost forever."

Despite the almost compulsive search for origin and identity displayed by the stories within this novel, each quest in its own way repudiates the existence of its goal. For example, although Suyuan claims that the East is where all begins, we learn that this "East" is not static; in fact, it moves and changes just as her Kweilin story changes each time she tells it. Although June takes her mother's place on the East side of the mahjong table, the East shifts places: "Auntie Ying throws the dice and I'm told that Auntie Lin has become the East wind. I've become the North wind, the last hand to play. Auntie Ying is the South and Auntie An-Mei is the West." Similarly, An-Mei learns that underneath the multiple layers of memory that compose one's sense of self, there is no authentic core: "you must peel off your skin, and that of your mother, and her mother before her. Until there is nothing. No scar, no skin, no flesh." And Ying Ying finds that although as she ages she feels closer and "closer to the beginning" of her life, that beginning, that origin is fluid—not fixed, but variable. She suggests this fluidity in speaking of the traumatic day in her childhood when she falls from a boat and is separated from her family. This moment in her life comes to represent, for her, the origin of her loss of self and the beginning, in a sense, of her adult life: "And I remember everything that happened that day because it has happened many times in my life. The same innocence, trust, and restlessness; the wonder, fear, and loneliness. How I lost myself." Further undermining any sense of fixed origins, Ying Ying's beginning also represents an end, a loss; for her, coming to a recognition of one's self entails a loss of a sense of wholeness. The quests embarked upon by these women, therefore, repudiate the ability to recover any type of static identity which might solidify exclusionary conceptions of gendered and racialized subjectivity; at the same time, however, they stress the importance of the histories of these characters to their ongoing sense of agency, highlighting an idea of history as not completely knowable, but nevertheless significant to the discursive construction of identity.

Empowerment Through Woman-to-Woman Bonding

Leslie Bow

Leslie Bow has taught at Brown University and the University of Wisconsin-Madison. She is the author of Betrayal and Other Acts of Subversion: Feminism, Sexual Politics, Asian American Women's Literature.

The popularity of The Joy Luck Club *has spurred interest in Asian American writing. But the novel's feminist message of empowerment through woman-to-woman bonding broadens its appeal beyond that of an ethnic work of literature. Tan's second-generation women, the daughters, view themselves in terms of their connections with others and strive for individuality. Their mothers pass on to them lessons about feminine strength and resolve so that their battle to free themselves from the mothers' grip is replaced by their awareness of how similar they are to the older generation. The daughter's ethnic conflicts are subordinated to their creation of bonds with other women, and in this manner they resolve their struggles for identity.*

If you really want to learn how to act Chinese, go live with a Chinese mother for twenty years. Then you'll act Chinese.

—Amy Tan

One of the lines highlighted in an early review of Amy Tan's *The Joy Luck Club* set off warning lights for me: "Once you are born Chinese, you cannot help but feel and think Chinese." Now I am Chinese, but I do not know what it means to "feel and think Chinese." As an academic I can question this equation of knowledge and biology in the same way that feminists question feminine essence. But my discomfort goes beyond academics. To take off on the phrase, "It's a Black thing, you wouldn't understand," if feeling and thinking Chinese is a Chinese thing and *I* didn't understand, where did that leave me?

More significantly, I approached the novel with some suspicion, wondering if this hint of delving into the mysteries of an inscrutable Chinese essence were in part the reason for the novel's mainstream appeal. Did Amy Tan, like Jade Snow Wong [American ceramicist and author], see herself as a cultural tour guide?

As evidenced by Tan's $4 million advance for *The Kitchen God's Wife* following the commercial success of *The Joy Luck Club*, Asian American literature is currently a "hot property." Yet this interest in the market value of ethnic fiction, of books "riding on the hyphen" or crossing over to a mainstream audience, brings with it a set of problematic issues about the authors' presentation of their material, how works are sold, and how they are interpreted. Part of the tension is in the categorization of certain works of fiction as "Asian American" at all. For writers who simultaneously claim a space within a currently recognizeable market while insisting on their own autonomy as artists, this poses a particular problem. [Japanese American novelist] Cynthia Kadohata notes, "My writing has a very strong and definite Asian sensibility, but I don't think a writer should be pigeonholed as an 'Asian American writer.'" Gus Lee's statement of autonomy ironically carries ethnic overtones: "We're all individual writers ... It would be awful if we were compressed into one single dumpling."

Given this sudden attention to Asian American literature by major publishing houses, my concern as a critic is, "Why *this* work and not *that* one?" Why do works like *The Joy Luck Club* or [Gus Lee's novel] *China Boy* garner mainstream attention while a vast number of others do not? Literary merit *might* be too easy an answer because aesthetics has just as often been invoked as a criterion for exclusion from the canon as a reason for inclusion. Mainstream interest in works by ethnic authors has always been ideologically loaded. What images of America's racial Other have been privileged by the Book of the Month Club, and how can one begin to make connections between marketability and racial representation within the dominant culture? As a bestselling "ethnic" text, *The Joy Luck Club* provides an interesting case of "universality" and cultural particularity.

Feminist Bonding

I want to suggest that Tan's "universal" appeal is more complex than her simple capitulation to an Orientalist discourse. She avoids discomfiting a mainstream readership with expressions of Chinese cultural nationalism or overtly politicized content but does not entirely resort to an easy and familiar essentializing of ethnicity. Rather, she is able to avoid difficult questions of race and ethnicity through her displacement of a cultural conflict to a feminist one. In *The Joy Luck Club*, the cultural distance between immigrant mothers and American-born daughters becomes resolved not through the characters' confrontation with contrasting cultural values but through their recognition that a matrilineal heritage transcends the generation gap caused by the daughters' integration into American culture.

The Joy Luck Club represents one aspect of feminism— that of the possibility of women's empowerment through the affirmation of a woman-to-woman bond. June's four stories set up an initial conflict that the stories of Waverly, Lena, and Rose echo: "My mother and I never really understood one another." Tan's emphasis on the mother/daughter bond invites a feminist reading based on two paradigms: June and Waverly must reconcile their belief that they cannot live up to their mothers' expectations, and Lena and Rose must learn strength from their maternal inheritance. The conflict set up in June's first story, that "my mother and I spoke two different languages," is not shown to be a literal disjunction between Chinese and English as indicative of a cultural gap, but a metaphoric gap based on her inability to "translate" her mother's meanings.

The novel displaces culture as the source of conflict by posing the question of the daughters' ethnic self-construction as a matter of their struggle for self autonomy either through or against their mothers who are constructed as the location of whatever is "Chinese" within themselves. The negotiation of the daughters' assimilation into American culture is played out generationally in terms of their relationship to their mothers as the transmitters of Chinese culture. In this sense, *The Joy Luck Club* locates questions of the daughters' resolution between tensions of assimilation and cultural nationalism, their ambivalence towards the mothers' challenge to their ethnic authenticity, "How do you know what is Chinese, what is not Chinese?" within the mother/daughter bond.

Here, I first want to develop a feminist reading of the novel based on [feminist sociologist and psychoanalyst] Nancy Chodorow's psychoanalytic model of gendered personality, then to problematize this reading based solely on gender by suggesting that it is through gender issues that ethnic identity is negotiated, and finally to reflect upon the often contentious interpretive relationship between feminism and cultural nationalism. In arguing that Tan's conflict displacement may be linked to the novel's mainstream appeal, I want to reflect upon the connection between feminist and racial discourses in ethnic women's writing.

The Flexible Feminine Ego

Because the daughters' ethnicity is posed in terms of their connection with and need to separate from their mothers,

Chodorow's thesis on mother/daughter embeddedness has resonance for the relationships in Tan's novel. In "Family Structure and Feminine Personality," she theorizes the dynamics of the mother/daughter relationship through her concept of the feminine ego as flexible and embedded in contrast to a more individuated male ego. These masculine and feminine differences in "unconscious features of personality" are produced in child rearing practices, particularly through mothering. According to Chodorow, because as primary caretakers mothers tend to "identify more with daughters and help them to differentiate less . . . the processes of separation and individuation are made more difficult for girls." Because "a woman identifies with her own mother and, through identification with her child, she (re)experiences herself as a cared-for child," a mother is likely to "experience her daughter (or parts of her daughter's life) as herself." The consequence of a feminine ego based on connection and relation rather than autonomy and agency is boundary confusion with others, particularly with the mother. If "mature dependence" characterized by a strong sense of self and self-worth is not developed through strong kinship and real role expectations—as is likely in working class matrifocal societies—then the consequence of a woman's embedded ego is immature dependence characterized by the need to look to others for self-affirmation and self-esteem. All four of Tan's mothers reflect this connectedness with their daughters; all four daughters struggle with their ambivalence toward this dependence.

Strong Female Models

Tan's realization that "I learned at sixteen that I didn't ever want to live for the approval of others" becomes a lesson for her characters. In Chodorow's terms, June and Waverly's attempts to construct a version of themselves separate from their mothers' expectations and Lena and Rose's need to stand autonomously from their husbands reveal that they experience their flexible ego boundaries conflictually.

June and Waverly are presented with strong female models in their mothers Suyuan and Lindo. June experiences this model with a sense of self doubleness; her mother's version of her perfect self encroaches against her "true self."

> It was not only the disappointment my mother felt in me. In the years that followed. I failed her so many times, each time asserting my own will, my right to fall short of expectations . . . For unlike my mother, I did not believe I could be anything I wanted to be. I could only be me.

Suyuan's lost daughters in China become the imaginary embodiment of the perfect daughter that June, or for that matter, Tan herself, failed to be. Tan locates her story within family history—after her parents' immigration from China, they were separated from their three daughters by the revolution in 1949. The good daughter/bad daughter split was realized by her sisters' absence:

> Amy's mother remembered them as perfect babies, perfect little girls, and then over the years, they became the "good Chinese daughters," some kind of ideal. "And I—" Amy laughs. "I was definitely the *bad* Chinese daughter."

Negotiating between the two selves is a matter of reading the positive within her mother's meanings: "She always said things that didn't make any sense, that sounded both good and bad at the same time." Here, June does not negate this doubleness, but reverses its terms. Her struggle is not so much to divorce her sense of self from her mother's but to cultivate her ability to ascribe the positive interpretation to herself and accept it as her mother's interpretation. "Best Quality" reveals that while conceding that "June not sophisticate," her mother respects her daughter's giving and straightforward character. June's sense of "running to escape someone chasing (her) only to look behind and discover there was no one there" allows her to reconcile the fact that there is no "better self" seeking to overwhelm her by reminding her of her own limitations, that the selves characterized by her two recital pieces "Pleading Child" and "Perfectly Content" are "two halves of the same song." While the first story introduces her hesitation to take her mother's place at Joy Luck, her unresolved feeling that she cannot be her mother, June's resolution comes when she realizes that her mother is yet "in her blood."

In "Rules of the Game," Waverly's conflict over her mother's "bragging" about her chess championships arises out of Waverly's need to individuate herself by claiming her accomplishments as her own. Her later stories reveal that she is dependent upon her mother's approval for her own self-esteem. Waverly's belief that her mother "never thinks anybody is good enough for anything" causes her to develop her own strategies and scenarios aimed at eliciting her mother's approval. Like June, Waverly's reconciliation comes not out of negating her embeddedness but through a reversal of subject positions with her mother. She can see herself as a "scared child" and view her mother, not as an enemy with secret weapons, but merely as "an old woman . . . getting a little crabby as she waited patiently for her daughter to invite her in." She makes peace with herself not through the recognition that she is a person autonomous from her mother, but through the opposite, that she is more like her mother than she realized.

Stand Tall and Listen to Your Mother

Lena and Rose's stories operate on a related paradigm. Unlike Waverly and June whose issues of embeddedness concern their relationship to their mothers, Lena and Rose are shown to be dependent upon their husbands to the extent that they lack the will to stand up for themselves. They recognize that their sense of self as undeserving is "commonplace in women like us." Because the mothers Ying Ying and An-mei see this as an unfortunate consequence of their maternal inheritance, they accept responsibility to remedy their daughters' lack of spirit. An-mei believes that Rose's lack of faith in her own agency derives from a mixture of genetic inheritance and feminine conditioning directly related to mothering:

> I was taught to desire nothing, to swallow other people's misery, to eat my own bitterness. And even though I taught my daughter the opposite, still she came out the same way! Maybe it is because she was born to me and she was born a girl. And I was born to my mother and I was born a girl.

If one subordinates the self to others—in Chodorow's terms, "immature dependence," in An-mei and Ying Ying's "born without wood" or having no *chi*—the remedy presented in the novel is to "stand tall and listen to your mother standing next to you." The result is not so much a transferral of dependence as the mothers' desire to pass on a feminist lesson of strength gained through their own losses and suffering: An-mei's stories of her disgraced mother's suicide reveal that a woman's only power lay in self-renunciation; Ying Ying's stories deal with her increasing dysfunction which she experiences as a loss of self. Both Ying Ying and An-mei put their knowledge of the limiting roles of women into the service of their daughters who, despite class and cultural differences, are yet subject to the same male expectations of women's subordination. Unlike Lindo whose stories suggest her skill in subverting her arranged marriage ("I started to think about how I would escape this marriage without breaking my promise to my family") and her "devious" manipulation in soliciting a chosen marriage proposal, Ying Ying and An-mei's capitulation to "fate" rather than their "faith" in changing their situations serves as a warning to their daughters.

While these lessons are derived from the mothers' social experience as women in China, their faith in the lessons' transference is attributed to the blood tie. Throughout *The Joy Luck Club*, the maternal connection is mystified as a genetic inheritance. An-mei's comment "A mother knows what is inside you" derives from her belief that one's own true nature, "what was beneath my skin. Inside my bones," lies within "her mother and her mother before her." Ying Ying's sense that the self/other split is never entirely broken with a daughter is echoed in her comment, "She and I have shared the same body. There is a part of her mind that is a part of mine. But when she was born, she sprang from me like a slippery fish, and has been swimming away ever since." Similarly, the mothers counter fears that their daughters do not know them and cannot pass their "truths and hopes" on to succeeding generations by exclaiming upon what should be obvious: "Not know your own mother? . . . Your mother is in your bones!" The novel's resolution for all the daughters is echoed in June's ending realization that "I also see what part of me is Chinese. It is so obvious. It is my family. It is in our blood."

A Neat, Feminist Ending

The daughters' embrace of blood ties as a means of reconciling the mother/daughter bond gives the novel its overly neat, feminist ending—the battle for autonomy from one's mother, one's difference from her, is replaced with the recognition of one's sameness to her. This similarity finds its basis in facial features, family, mutual respect of character, and the trials of acceding to the secondary role of women in marriage. Yet Tan's emphasis on the woman-to-woman bond obscures the generational differences between immigrant mothers and assimilated daughters. This is partially effected through Tan's construction of the Chinese mother as the embodiment of the Chinese half of the daughters' cultural hybridity as Chinese Americans. The daughters' racial identity is played out against the figure of the mother who stands in for the daughters' sense of racial and cultural difference within themselves. Thus their ambivalence toward their own ethnicity is played out in their relationships with their mothers. . . .

Feminine Strength as Maternal Inheritance

Throughout *The Joy Luck Club*, the mother/daughter distance takes the form of the daughters' devaluation of what they perceive as foreign in their mothers as a means of substantiating their own American-ness. The disassociation they effect is not only in terms of individuation of the child from the mother but also in terms of the formation of the daughters' national identity through their disassociation from immigrant parents.

The daughters' racial consciousness, "what it means to be Chinese," occurs not necessarily as their ability to claim racial identity through the recognition of how it is constituted as Other within the dominant culture, but as their new ability to valorize what is Chinese in their mothers and to claim it as their own. Yet in Tan's novel, the reconciliation of a cultural dichotomy is effected through a recognition of *feminine* strength as a "natural" maternal inheritance.

Feminist Resolution Trumps Racial Differences

The Joy Luck Club is an aesthetically pleasing novel: its resolution satisfyingly complete. Its convincing and humorous portrayal of the relationship between mothers and daughters is an important part of its emotional resonance. Tan's novel highlights the complex, often ambivalent relationship between mothers and daughters and an important source of women's community. An accessible work, it is easy to "relate to" given the apparent universality of the mother/daughter experience. Additionally, the positive effect of having Amy Tan's voice out in a mainstream literary market . . . cannot be denied.

However, the content and circumstances surrounding *The Joy Luck Club* can suggest larger issues about ideological interpretation and the dissemination of Asian American literary texts. *The Joy Luck Club* seems eminently marketable because it presents American ethnic angst as privatized and familial, and thereby addresses issues of race in a non-threatening manner. This is not to critique the text for what it is not, but it is fair to pose the question, "How will Tan's success affect subsequent Asian American writers who might hold more overtly political or culturally nationalist views?" In being seen as less commodifiable, will they get "Amy Tan" rejection slips like those that exhort budding writers to "write more like [novelist Maxine Hong] Kingston"? Also, because Tan's book lends itself to feminist interpretation, will it be subject to white feminist coopting, readings that continually foreground questions of gender over those of racial identity? . . .

By containing a racial discourse within a feminist one, Tan's novel allows her characters to reach identity resolution without confronting their racial difference. Instead, the novel mystifies racial subject formation by portraying it as a matter of blood ties and displacing it onto what Alice Walker praises on the book jacket as "the mystery of the mother-daughter bond." Given the ease of her introduction into the literary marketplace—perhaps attributable to a narrative "sneak attack" in containing questions of ethnic difference within a "universal" feminist resolution—Amy Tan may have been following the advice of one of her characters: "Wise guy, he not go against wind . . . Strongest wind cannot be seen."

Asian American Gender Stereotypes in *The Joy Luck Club*

Yuan Shu

Yuan Shu is assistant professor of English at Texas Tech University. He teaches contemporary American literature and Asian American studies.

American readers may understand ethnic novels such as The Joy Luck Club *through the lens of their own perceptions of Asian culture, particularly with regard to masculine and feminine stereotypes about Asians. Students wonder why Tan seems to reinforce certain negative stereotypes about Asian men and women; ethnic writers, they believe, must be mindful of the consequences of their writing strategies. Tan is nevertheless highly successful in appealing to a mainstream American audience, but the audience's notion of Asian values in the novel is an ever-changing one that often depends on how a particular reader interprets the text.*

When I was teaching Amy Tan's *The Joy Luck Club*, a work my students enjoyed reading and writing about, I spent much time with them discussing the significance of the introductory vignette and the meaning of the swan as a metaphor in the book. One student interpreted the vignette as Tan's means of establishing the tone of the story and considered the swan as a symbol of the dream of the old Chinese immigrant woman coming to America and seeking a better life for herself and her daughter. When the immigration officials pulled the swan away from the woman, she added, the

Yuan Shu, "Globalization and 'Asian Values': Teaching and Theorizing Asian American Literature," *College Literature*, vol. 32, winter 2005, pp. 86–101. Copyright © 2005 by West Chester University. Reproduced by permission.

swan then became the site of tension between the dream of the immigrant woman and the reality of a racialized America, a tension that would transform the feather of the swan from a simple object of memory to a loaded representation of Chinese values. The student concluded that Tan considers assimilation as the key to success in American culture and society when she mentions Coca-Cola and perfect American English repeatedly in the vignette, but she still thinks that Chinese values should play a role in helping to fulfill the American Dream. What puzzled the student, however, was Tan's statement that a woman's worth in China "is measured by the loudness of her husband's belch" in the vignette. Why does Tan represent Chinese culture in this seemingly humorous but actually superficial way? How do we know what "Chinese values" are represented authentically in the text?

Questioning Chinese Values

Rather than answering these questions from the outset and addressing Tan's strategy in representing "Chinese values," I decided to defer them for the moment and solicited more responses from students. Most students had not thought much about Tan's way of representing "Chinese values," but instead they identified themselves with the second-generation daughters in terms of the point of view. They interpreted the mother-daughter relationship in the first narrative titled "The Joy Luck Club" as a power struggle between the mother as a "control freak" who showed no sign of compassion or understanding of her child and the daughter as an Americanized woman who had tried to articulate her own freedom and independence without following her parent's guide or advice. When I asked how the mother tried to control the daughter, students responded by stating that the mother did so by disseminating "Chinese values" to the daughter. As I told students to locate and explain those values, they noticed that "Chinese values" in the text were actually flexible in the way the mother introduced them and interpreted their meanings. One student speculated that this flexibility revealed the fact that these values were highly selective rather than randomly introduced and were meant to serve the mother's purpose in manipulating the daughter rather than getting any cultural message across.

While students were still debating whether the mother was manipulative or simply defensive in her new cultural environment, I called their attention to the fact that it was usually at the moment when the mother lost her sense of parental authority over her young, Americanized daughter as an inarticulate and incompetent Asian immigrant in the American context that she started preaching "Chinese values." Some students followed this line and suggested that teaching and promoting "Chinese values" were probably her only means of showing her cultural competence and authority in front of her Americanized daughter, whose thinking and behavior had been defined and endorsed by the dominant culture. Others argued that those "Chinese values" were actually the mother's personal values that she had gained from her own unfortunate experience in Chinese culture over the years and that she had really meant to help her daughter to substantiate her American Dream, which she herself would never be able to achieve because of her language and cultural barriers. Still others concluded that there were more similarities than differences between the mother and the daughter in the sense that the former had rebelled against her mother in Chinese society in exactly the same way that the latter had done to hers in American society. Students then returned to the initial question: what are "Chinese values"?

As we read more narratives told from the first person point of view of the immigrant mothers, I asked students to compare Tan's work with Maxine Hong Kingston's *The Woman Warrior*, which we had read early in the semester. One student argued that Tan had done a fairer job by allowing the immi-

A student in an English class at the Commodore Stockton School in San Francisco's Chinatown neighborhood, during the 1950s. Orlando/Hulton Archive/Getty Images.

grant mother to develop her own voice and giving us an opportunity to see the similarities and differences between the immigrant mother and the American daughter in different contexts whereas Kingston subjected the mother entirely to the opinionated interpretation and speculation of the daughter as the narrator of *The Woman Warrior*. The difference between these two strategies, she agreed further, was that the daughter's behavior and thought in Kingston's work were understood not just as Asian American but also as the perfect American norm whereas the daughter's comments and reactions in Tan's novel were actually put into some kind of perspective. A second student proposed that the mother in Kingston's work was contradictorily positioned because she sent her daughter confusing messages about the patriarchal system, whereas the mothers in Tan's work were more consistent when they taught their daughters why they themselves had rebelled against the Chinese patriarchal culture and how they had succeeded in developing their own voices. A third student recapitulated our class discussion by suggesting that the values in Tan's novel were both "Chinese" and "American." He elaborated his point by stating that the mothers and daughters in Tan's work had shared the same values that had worked in both Chinese and American contexts because both generations would speak up for their own minds, fight for their own rights, and work for their own dreams regardless of the hostile social and political circumstances. He concluded that these were exactly fundamental American values and ethics. In exploring "Chinese values" from concrete forms to abstract notions, students had finally passed the stage of looking for values and focused more on the appropriation of values and the context in which the values were situated.

Stereotypes in Ethnic Fiction

After we unveiled the possible layers of the meanings that had been related to the "Chinese values" in Tan's *Joy Luck Club*, we returned to the question that the woman student had brought up on the first day of our class discussion, which concentrated on Tan's strategy of representation in the introductory vignette. Most students interpreted it as a writing strategy that had meant to appeal to the broader audiences in the United States and had served her purposes very well in that regard. One student stated that as a creative writer, Tan should write on whatever she felt comfortable with and select whatever details she considered appropriate. He added that he had not had any problem with scenes such as the one in which the Chinese daughter cut her own flesh to brew soup and save the life of her dying mother even though he felt such a description was a little goofy and weird. Then one African American woman student challenged the argument by comparing the flesh-cutting scene to one episode in Toni Morrison's award-winning novel, *Beloved*, in which some black male slaves were described as having sexual intercourse with cows on the southern plantation. She argued that she understood that such things could have happened under the special social, cultural, and historical circumstances and should have been employed to demonstrate the humanity of black men, but such a description would equally reinforce the stereotypes concerning African American males in American culture and society today. She concluded that writers, minorities and women particularly, should always have in mind the consequences of their writing strategies. Finally, a third student defended Tan by pointing out a specific paragraph in the novel, in which the narrator challenged the stereotype of Asian women aging well and of Asian Americans as being perpetual foreigners in the country, and suggested that the flesh-cutting scene could prove Tan's candor and openness about her own cultural heritage. She concluded that she came to realize that the second generation Chinese American women had shared more things with her as a Euro-American woman than with their own immigrant mothers as Chinese women. That showed exactly what being an American had meant and what the American Dream had been all about.

A Range of Interpretations

As we were finishing our discussion on Tan's work, I introduced [critic] Sau-ling Wong's critique of *Joy Luck CLub*, [In "'Sugar Sisterhood': Situating the Amy Tan Phenomenon"] which highlights both the Orientalist and anti-Orientalist elements in the same work. Wong observed that "cultural mediation of the Orient for the 'mainstream' readership requires continual repackaging to remain in sync with changing times and resultant shifts in ideological needs". Though most students recognized that such "repackaging" might be Tan's way of marketing her work and herself, they concluded that it was the most American way to fulfill her own American Dream. They drew the conclusion that authors should educate their readers and challenge their intellectual abilities rather than simply pleasing and entertaining them.

In exposing students to different issues and controversies that surround Amy Tan's work, I realized that they actually deconstructed the "Asian values" that they had been preoccupied with and even recognized their own positions in interpreting this Asian American text. Even though these students did not necessarily change their attitude toward the radical critique of Asian American intellectuals, they at least understood "where that critique had come from" as one student put it, and how Asian American texts could be interpreted in different ways.

Tan Portrays Strong Asian Women

Jean Lau Chin

Jean Lau Chin has served as systemwide dean of the California School of Professional Psychology at Alliant International University in San Francisco. She is a licensed psychologist.

Classic Chinese stories tend to emphasize the mother-son relationship, while traditional Western fairy tales often cast the mother in the role of a villain in competition with the daughter. The Joy Luck Club realistically portrays the mother-daughter relationship as one of both bonding and bondage. The story of An-mei Hsu and her children casts the mother in the traditional role of rescuer, while that of Lindo Jong and Waverly portrays the mother as an intrinsically strong woman warrior. The book's depiction of strong Asian women is a welcome change from the many Western stories, such as Miss Saigon, *which show Asian women in weak and subservient roles.*

Stories of mother-daughter bonds are more abundant in contemporary literature, coinciding with the women's movement. The connection among women in their relationships is celebrated. Classic Chinese stories tend to emphasize the closeness of the mother-son relationship together with themes of family obligation and loyalty.

Triumph of the Daughter in Western Fairy Tales

Classic Western fairy tales typically portray the mother as the villain, and the mother-daughter relationship as competitive, where the daughter replaces or is triumphant over the mother

Jean Lau Chin, *Learning from My Mother's Voice: Family Legend and the Chinese American Experience*. New York: Teachers College Press, 2005. Copyright © 2005 by Teachers College, Columbia University. All rights reserved. Reproduced by permission.

figure. Snow White, for example, is about an adolescent girl beset by a jealous stepmother, the queen, who tries to destroy her because she is more beautiful. When the queen issues an order to kill her, the servants instead abandon her in the forest, thus saving her life. When the queen again tries to destroy her, the dwarfs rescue her. She finally succumbs to a deathlike sleep after tempted with a poisoned apple from the stepmother. A handsome prince falls in love with her beauty and rescues her. During the journey, the poisoned apple is jarred loose and Snow White regains consciousness. The queen dies (from jealousy), and the couple live happily ever after.

Cinderella, another favorite Western fairy tale, is about a beautiful, patient, and modest adolescent girl who is forced to perform menial tasks and is rejected by her two spoiled, haughty, and heartless stepsisters. After Cinderella's mother dies, her father marries a cruel stepmother who is jealous of her beauty as an emerging adolescent. Unbeknownst to her stepmother and stepsisters, Cinderella attends the 3-day celebration as a princess, during which the prince becomes enthralled with her. In her haste to leave the ball before midnight to avoid being transformed back to her original self in rags, she loses her glass slipper. The prince sets out to find his true love and the rightful owner of this slipper.

Like many Western fairy tales, there is competition and heightened rivalry between mother and daughter over who is more beautiful. The 3 days symbolize three stages of maturation or developmental tasks that Cinderella must go through before she can achieve the maturity and integration of self to meet her prince face-to-face. The mother figure is typically split. In the story of Snow White, the good pre-Oedipal mother—that is, the all-giving, all protecting mother—dies early in the story while the bad Oedipal mother (i.e., the depriving, selfish, rejecting, and unjust mother), represented by the jealous queen, tries to deny the heroine an independent existence. The father is mostly absent and unable to rescue or to protect Snow White, for she must journey on her own. These fairy tales portray females in passive and receptive roles with characters of innocence and beauty; they are victim to the external forces besetting them in a journey of sexual maturation, and of separation and independence; they need to be rescued by a charming prince.

Bonds and Bondage in *The Joy Luck Club*

The Joy Luck Club, a contemporary novel by Amy Tan, is about the lives of four Chinese American immigrant women and their daughters. The portraits of the intergenerational relationships illustrate the influence of culture and immigration on the psychological adjustment of the characters. They are slaves to their past, a fact that both bonds them together and puts them in bondage. Historical Chinese culture and themes in this contemporary novel celebrate women as nurturing mothers and capture the struggles, developmental crises, and character transformations of these women in evolving a bicultural identity. Two of the mother-daughter relationships are chosen for analysis here because they represent the rescue fantasy and warrior image of women, so characteristic in the fairy tales and myths being discussed.

An-Mei Hsu and the Rescue Fantasy

The character of An-Mei Hsu portrays the rescue fantasy, the bondage of fate, and how the theme of separation and abandonment is recurrent through several generations in her family. Born of the element water (symbolic of women), she is raised by her grandmother because her mother brought shame to the family. According to family lore, her mother ran off to marry a rich man after her husband died. An-Mei later discovers that her mother was actually raped as a ruse to dishonor her and force her to marry this man in order to bear him a son. Her mother returns to the dying grandmother; she cuts a piece of her flesh to be boiled in a medicinal soup, symbolic of the highest sacrifice of a daughter to her mother in a consciously fruitless attempt to heal. The boiling water scars An-Mei as she rushes to join her mother against her grandmother's wishes. She almost dies of suffocation, and it is only the grandmother's threat of abandonment that brings her back. An-Mei's mother later commits suicide (i.e., once again abandoning her) as the only way she knows to guarantee An-Mei's safe status in her husband's household; her husband was forced to honor An-Mei forever or run the risk of retribution and wrath from her mother's spirit. In doing so, she achieved for her daughter through her death what she could not do in her life.

A motto in Chinese society is that it is better to die with honor than to live with shame. During Confucian [based on the teachings of ancient Chinese philosopher Confucius] society, a woman's sanctity and honor belonged to her husband; rape marked the defilement of women's honor. During an era when women were without choices, it was not uncommon for women to choose suicide as a means of regaining their honor.

The myth in An-Mei's family is that "an ancestor once stole water from a sacred well, and now water steals her son away." This is An-Mei's explanation when her daughter's inattention results in her son being drowned at sea on a family outing. (It also symbolizes the family curse, because her mother's rape brought shame to the family; she is then rejected, in the tradition of blaming women as sexual seducers while forgiving men for their impulsiveness and carnal desires.) An-Mei brings out the family Bible in a consciously fruitless attempt to bring her son back; she cries in despair for being so foolish to think she could use faith to change fate.

An-Mei rescues her daughter from her marriage to a white dermatologist. Her daughter, Rose, spends 17 years in a dependent and unhealthy marriage whereby her husband constantly rescues her emotionally. In despair over her failing marriage and impending divorce, Rose attempts suicide. As

An-Mei helps her daughter heal from her psychological pain, she is able to resolve her own issues of separation and abandonment. Mother and daughter plant a seedling together, nourished by water, symbolic of their new start. Rose is able to move from dependency to a healthy interdependence with her mother.

Lindo Jong as Woman Warrior

The character of Lindo Jong in *The Joy Luck Club* offers a somewhat different portrayal of Chinese American women, more similar to the classic Chinese story of Hua Mu Lan, the Woman Warrior. Worried that her grandchildren will forget her, Lindo's mother gives her a gold bracelet, symbolic of the purity and genuineness of Chinese culture and character. Born without metal but of good character, Lindo comes from a poor upbringing, and is married into a well-to-do family at age 16 when her family is forced to leave (i.e., abandoning her) because of the floods. The marriage is loveless and is not consummated. Unable to produce an heir, Lindo is blamed by her mother-in-law for being too balanced with the metal— meaning the gold, which she brought with her to the marriage.

Given that divorce was taboo during these times, Lindo cunningly devises a way to capitalize on her in-laws' superstitious beliefs and fears of social taboo. She fabricates a vision using information that she has astutely observed to predict that her marriage is doomed unless it is immediately dissolved. Her in-laws believe her vision; they are all too willing to help her leave the household to avoid the bad omen and fate predicted by her vision to befall her husband. Thus, she is freed from her marriage without shame or ostracism; her in-laws gratefully send her away to Beijing if she promises not to tell her story, an unusual accomplishment during those times in China. It is her cleverness, resoluteness, and being true to herself that carry her through.

Lindo's daughter, Waverly, is considered crafty and snobbish like her mother. She is taught the "art of invisible strength" by her mother; that is, that the inner will is a dominant force. The mother-daughter relationship is a battle of the wills. As Lindo says, the strongest wind cannot be seen (referring to the winds in mahjong and martial arts). Waverly continues a silent battle with her mother over independence. Waverly develops her skills as a champion chess player in which she learns secret strategies from a neighbor. As she competes in tournaments and becomes the neighborhood heroine, she believes she is special (which is in contrast to the emphasis on modesty in Chinese culture). However, she is resentful of her mother's pride as an attempt to take credit for her accomplishments. When her mother modestly describes her winning as "luck," she views this as criticism.

She rebels after a confrontation, only to lose her mother's silent support. Without her mother's support, she gives up the chess game and loses interest in winning. She finally comes to terms with her battle for independence from her mother, realizing it has been a battle fought within herself. What she saw "as a formidable foe in her mother, was now simply an old woman waiting for her daughter to come home."

Lindo and her daughter Waverly are born with the elements of wind—symbolizing strategy and invisible strength; their relationship emphasizes power and competition. Lindo's developmental transformation is her ability to give up the fight with her mother.

A Truer Depiction of Motherhood

This contemporary novel of women in Chinese immigrant families differs from their depiction in classical Chinese stories in that it portrays mothers as human beings with faults. Its portrayal of mother-daughter bonds also differs from the ten-dency to portray cross-gender parent-child relationships (father-daughter, mother-son, and husband-wife) in classical Chinese stories.

In *The Joy Luck Club*, Chinese culture continues to pervade the characters' lives while creating conflict with the influence of American culture in their lives. The Chinese American mothers continue to use Confucian moral principles and threats in their childrearing techniques. Lindo uses open criticism of Waverly's accomplishment—a common demonstration of Chinese modesty—to elicit compliments; Waverly misunderstands her mother's maternal pride and modesty as simple criticism, illustrating a common intergenerational misunderstanding in immigrant families. . . .

[T]he emphasis on maternal guidance is cause for tension between mothers and daughters in *The Joy Luck Club*. As the daughters in this novel struggle for autonomy and identity, they rebel against maternal guidance and control. The mothers cannot understand the daughters' failure to abide by the mandate to be the obedient daughter.

Each generation grapples with the same dynamic issues faced by their mothers before—symbolized by the elements with which they were born and that determine their fate. Despite their initial disdain and rebelliousness against maternal expectations, the daughters come to realize how perceptive their mothers are and come to value what they have gained. The process is transforming in establishing their bicultural identity and mother-daughter bonds.

The themes of loss and abandonment in An-Mei's story and the warrior images in Lindo's story are powerful cultural symbols and developmental themes as each negotiates the task of maturation.

Western Myths of Asian Women

The contemporary portrayals of Chinese American women in *The Joy Luck Club* are . . . popular among Chinese Americans because they emphasize women's strengths and end with admiration and pride, unlike many portrayals popular among Westerners about Asian women, including *Madame Butterfly*, *Sayonara*, and *Miss Saigon*, which portray Asian women as meek, subservient, and victimized. The latter stories end with pity for the heroine; they are tragedies whereby the Asian woman typically commits suicide following her unfulfilled union with the white male—that is, Asian women are abandoned and shamed. These stories mimic Asian values and are written from Western perspectives. Westerners often fail to understand that the latter portrayals victimize Asian women and deifies white men.

Other 20th-century stories about Asian women featured them as prostitutes and losers. These were initially popular among Asian audiences because so few movies featured Asian women as stars; they were later seen as offensive because they reinforced stereotypic myths and images about Asian women as subservient, exotic, and self-effacing while remaining immensely popular among Western audiences.

Social Issues
in Literature

CHAPTER 3

Contemporary Perspectives on Women's Issues

Mothers Are Society's Scapegoats

Paula Caplan

Paula Caplan is the author of Don't Blame Mother: Mending the Mother-Daughter Relationship *and* They Say You're Crazy: How the World's Most Powerful Psychiatrists Decide Who's Normal.

Despite the advances women have made in the feminist era, mothers are still blamed for a wide range of problems in today's society. When children act out, it is more likely to be the mothers who shoulder the blame, even in two-parent families. Scholarly studies often ignore important factors in pinning blame on motherhood, and society accepts these criticisms because of the need for a convenient scapegoat. It is no more acceptable to blame mothers for all problems than it is to blame women for society's ills, and women need to speak up in defense of mothers.

I became interested in mother blaming when I was working in a clinic where we were evaluating families. I noticed that no matter what was wrong, no matter what the reason for the family's coming to the clinic, it turned out that the mother was always assumed to be responsible for the problem. And if, in the assessment interview, she sat right next to the child, my colleagues would say afterward, "Did you see how she sat right next to the child? She is smothering and overcontrolling and too close and enmeshed and symbiotically fused with the child." But if she did not sit right next to the child, she was called cold and rejecting—and, if the child was a boy, castrating.

The Persistence of Mother-Blame

So my interest in mother blaming began because it seemed that there was nothing that a mother could do that was right, and it was particularly interesting and painful to me because I myself was a mother.

In 1986, when I received tenure and considered what I most wanted to teach, one of the two courses I created was about mothers. I wasn't aware at the time of any other course about mothers, so I started trying to design the course and talking to people about it. Often, both men and women would laugh and say, "What are you going to talk about for a whole semester?" or just, "Hah! A course about mothers?" You may remember a similar reaction people had ten years earlier to "Oh! You're going to have a course about women?"

Teaching that course to graduate students at the University of Toronto's Ontario Institute for Studies in Education led to my writing *Don't blame mother*. In the book, I describe aspects of girls' and women's socialization that create or exacerbate problems between mothers and daughters, as well as methods that mothers and daughters have found helpful in repairing rifts between them. (I did not believe and still do not believe that the mother-daughter relationship is more fraught with problems than the mother-son relationship, or the relationships between fathers and their children of either sex. However, as a feminist I was primarily concerned with the kinds of socially created—and, therefore, hopefully surmountable—barriers between women.) In addressing the question "To what extent is the content of *Don't blame mother* applicable today?" I find it depressing that most of the basic principles that concerned me as I wrote the book still apply today. . . .

After my experience in the clinical setting described earlier, I did some research with Ian Hall-McCorquodale, looking at articles in clinical journals written by psychoanalysts, psychiatrists, social workers, psychologists, behavior therapists, and clinicians of all stripes. We found that mothers were blamed for virtually every kind of psychological or emotional problem that ever brought any patient to see a therapist. We were also disappointed to find that the sex of the person who was writing the paper did not determine the presence or absence of mother blaming, and, even more depressingly, that it didn't get better as the years passed after the resurgence of the women's movement during the 1970s. With respect to mother blame, so many therapists still seemed to be buried under their rocks.

Lack of Appreciation

When I began to bring up this subject of mother blame I pointed out that there are myths about mothers that allow us to take anything a mother might do and turn it into evidence of something "bad" about her. Important work that a mother does goes largely unnoticed, except when she doesn't do it, as when she is sick and can't make dinner. I would point out that nobody I knew of was likely to say to their mother, "That was a great week's work of dusting you did," or "That was a week of delicious and nourishing meals that you prepared." When I would say this, people would laugh—and still do, in fact.

So we have to ask, "Why does this make us laugh? Would you laugh if I said, 'Dad, the lawn looks great now that you have mowed it?'" Nobody laughs at that. Why? Because we laugh at the unexpected. It is so unimaginable to us that anyone would express appreciation for, or a sense of valuing of, the work that mothers do as mothers and housekeepers and cooks and chauffeurs. So I used to talk about that. . . .

[Researcher] Arlie Hochschild points out that women increasingly spend time at paid work because they feel appreciated there. She says that even for relatively uninteresting work, such as factory work, women find work to be a greater source of self-esteem than home life. This was something that had concerned me years ago, because it seemed to me that, as in that story about no one thanking you for dusting, even if you work at a really boring, miserable job, every week or two somebody hands you a paycheque. The cheque might not be much, but it communicates the notion that somebody puts some value on the work that you do. And it's still no better in terms of mothering.

Good and Bad Mother Myths

At the heart of *Don't blame mother* are mother myths I call the "Good Mother Myths" and mother myths I call the "Bad Mother Myths." The Good Mother Myths set standards that no human being could ever match, such as that mothers are always, naturally, one hundred percent nurturant. We have a double standard. We don't have that kind of expectation of fathers. So, when, one percent of the time, mothers don't do what we wish they would do, we feel betrayed, because the myth is that they naturally are able to and, in fact, are desperate to be nurturant all the time. But when our fathers do anything nurturant, we feel that it is wonderful that Daddy did something like that. (Naturally, the answer is not to stop appreciating what fathers do but rather to be ready to give mothers equal credit when they are nurturant.)

The Bad Mother Myths allow us to take mothers' neutral or bad behavior—because mothers are human, so we do some bad things—or even mothers' good behavior, and transform it into further proof that mothers are bad. One example that disturbs me the most is the myth that mother-daughter closeness is sick, that it is a form of psychopathology. When *Don't blame mother* was first published, and I was doing media interviews, every woman interviewer would confess, with the microphone turned off, that she talked to her mother every day. I would ask her, "How do you feel afterward?" and the woman would reply, "Oh, great. My mother has a great sense of humor, and we are great friends, and we give each other

Thousands of women march before the U.S. Captiol in support of a woman's right to choose an abortion, April 25, 2004. Paul J. Richards/AFP/Getty Images.

advice." I would then ask her, "Do you have a partner?" "Yes." "Do you talk to them every day?" "Yes." "Does that embarrass you?" "No." And I would ask, "Well, then, why did you confess that you talk to your mother every day?" These women would reply that they worried that the daily talks with their mothers were signs that they hadn't "individuated" or "achieved autonomy" from their mothers, and if they had been in therapy they would say, "I know it means we're enmeshed or symbiotically fused." My point here is that anything associated with mothers becomes devalued and pathologized.

If you look at the myths about mothers, you find that some of them are mutually exclusive. One of the Bad Mother Myths is that mothers are an endless drain on our energy: just on the basis of strict physics principles alone, you cannot be constantly putting out force (nurturance), while constantly taking in force and energy as you are draining it from others. Another set of mutually exclusive myths involves the Good Mother Myth, according to which mothers naturally, perhaps for hormonal reasons, know everything they need to know about mothering, and the Bad Mother Myth, according to which mothers cannot raise emotionally healthy children without the advice of lots of experts.

Mothers as Scapegoats

I believe that these mutually exclusive myths continue to co-exist because every society needs scapegoated groups if the people in power want to maintain their power. What happens if I'm in the powerful group and some member of the scapegoated group does something good? Somebody might get the idea that the scapegoated people are not as bad as I portray them to be, and if that's the case, maybe I don't deserve to have all of the power I have. So I have to make sure there is a myth for every occasion, so that no matter what the members of that scapegoated group might do, I can transform it into further proof that they are wrong, bad, or pathological, and deserve to continue to have no power and be scapegoated. That is the powerful function that these myths serve, and that is why we need to keep questioning them.

This power hierarchy still exists, and the women's movement hasn't been able to change it yet. I think it hasn't changed partly because we often substitute the word *mother* for *woman*. For instance, people at a party may stop you when you tell a "joke" that is woman-hating, but if you change the word *woman* to *mother*, you can still get away with the comment. You are much less likely to have someone interrupt you to say, "I don't think that's funny, and I don't want you to go on like that."

What the women's movement can do is to make the repeated exposure of mother myths—the placing of them front and center—a priority. Anti-feminist backlash makes all feminist efforts more difficult, of course. But until we recognize the need for what we might call "the Norma Rae-ing of mothers' struggles, [after the rebellious hero of a popular movie]" the need to reveal mothers' oppression and its systemic nature, few women of any ethnic or racialized group or class or sexual orientation (and certainly not women with disabilities or women who don't weigh the "right" amount) will be free. Why? Because we all had mothers, and so we're connected with what is done to, what is said about mothers. Because we have all been subjected as women to strong pressure to prove we are unlike our mothers. You'll often hear women say, "My greatest fear is that I will be like my mother." What I find that these women usually mean if you explore that statement is, "I don't want to be treated the way she has been treated. I don't want to be demeaned and undervalued the way she is." At the same time as we are taught to not want to be like our mothers, we are taught—sometimes subliminally— that we should want to be like our mothers, when they are passive, pliable, and ashamed of themselves. And no one is free until the truths about mothers are highlighted, because all women, and especially as we age, are expected to be motherly, motherlike, as in being self-denying and serving others.

Superficial Studies Blame Mothers

No, it's not getting any better—not socially and not in the research arena. A recent issue of the *American Journal of Orthopsychiatry* includes a longitudinal report on "Preschool antecedents of adolescent assaultive behavior." The researchers studied children from preschool through adolescence in an attempt to discern the determinants of adolescents' assaultive behavior. How did they look at the alleged determinants? Among other things, they observed what they call early in their article "parental interactions" with the young children. That really meant "mothers' interactions," even though eighty-six percent of the children in their study had both a male and a female parent in the home. When they looked at how mothers interact with children, and then later on looked at which children become assaultive, it is not surprising that they concluded that it was the children's negative interactions with their mothers that led to their assaultive behavior.

The methodology you choose can go far to determine the results that you get. I believe that there are at least two major methodological problems evident in this study. One problem is not looking at the fathers or the society in which the children live, and what the determinants of their assaultive behavior might be. The second is a cause-effect problem. People who are assaultive when they are teenagers, for reasons that may have had nothing to do with their mothers, might have been difficult to handle as children, and thus their mothers' interactions with them would have been observed to be relatively "negative." For example, their mothers might have had to do more of the disciplining of them, more of the saying "no." That is just one example of the persistence of the practice of mother blame in "scholarly" journals. . . .

I hope that this sampling of the recent history of mother blame makes it clear that, despite some gains that feminists have made, there are still miles to go before we can relax in the knowledge that mother blame has been eradicated. For this reason, I suggest that we join together in declaring that women don't speak enough and don't speak up enough, certainly not in defense of mothers. Let us vow that at every possible opportunity we will protest, we will educate, even interrupt—as we would a sexist or a racist "joke"—when anyone in any setting utters or implies any of the dangerous myths about mothers.

Asian American Women Must Overcome Limiting Cultural Stereotypes

Nikki A. Toyama

Nikki A. Toyama is a graduate of Stanford University. She has worked as an engineer in Silicon Valley and for InterVarsity Christian Fellowship.

Walking through the red light districts of southeast Asia, one is struck by the sad spectacle of Asian women selling their bodies. There is an element in Asian culture that allows families to treat their female children in this degrading manner, while families in other cultures would never think of doing such a thing. Misogyny, or hatred of women, runs deep in Asia, and accounts for the limited status of Asian women. But Asian women are so much more than the sex objects or domestic servants that cultural stereotypes would have people believe.

I arrived in Thailand, the third leg of my trip. I had visited the urban slums of Cairo and Nairobi, and now I was in Bangkok. I was working on a project looking at the vulnerability of women among the urban poor. My project brought me to the red-light district of Bangkok.

I immediately felt at home in Thailand. The support railings in the trains stood at the perfect height for me to reach. I blended in with the crowd and fit in the local clothes sizes, and the food was amazing.

One day, while waiting for a friend, I sat on the steps outside a mall. Looking around, I noticed signs in Japanese and discreet entrances—the Japanese red-light district. This area catered to Japanese businessmen. We had been working, a few streets over, in the American red-light district. There Thai women catered to an American clientele. With my eyes now open, I began to notice other districts for German, British, French clients. Thai women were made available to all these men. I had no idea there was a district for each group. The streets extended for blocks—row after row of brothels and bars.

Feeling Violated

That night, I went back to the Japanese red-light district. I walked and asked God, "What do you want me to see?" I prayed for the women who worked in that area and for the men who were their patrons. I prayed for the wives and daughters of the men coming to these bars. I prayed against the broken systems in our society that promote and provide space for these industries. As I watched women call men into the bars, I prayed. After a couple of hours, I went home.

As I rode home on the train, I wondered what it meant for me, a Japanese American Christian. A Caucasian man approached me to ask a question. Before speaking, he looked over my body, from my legs to my face, though I was wearing very conservative missionary clothes. He was shameless. He did not try to mask his appraisal: he looked over my body as if assessing a product. I recognized this look—I had seen it repeatedly in the red-light district as the men entered the bars.

I had never felt so violated. The country marketed its sex industry too well, and I, though an outsider, felt its burden. Behaviors like freely staring at women's bodies were tolerated and promoted even. In that place, as an Asian woman, I was told, in effect, that my only contribution was as a sexual object.

I ran home from the train that night. I went to the room I shared with six others. Thankful that it was empty, I sat on my bed, a mat in the only air-conditioned corner of a slum church, and cried. I cried for myself, but then I cried for the women of Thailand.

Misogyny in Asia

I had visited urban slums in two other countries, Kenya and Egypt. Even though both places were significantly poorer (the monthly income in Nairobi was $30, Cairo $60, Bangkok $120), very few parents there would sell their little daughters into prostitution as parents do in Thailand. What makes a country and its families treat its women with so little regard? I thought of the women I met in the Kibera slum in Nairobi—as poor as they were, they would never sell their children.

Misogyny runs deep in Asia. Families abandon little baby girls in the Chinese countryside, waiting for a son. In Japan, college-educated girls are openly discriminated against in the workplace—they are passed over for promotions because it is assumed they will leave the workplace once they marry. The sex trade in Asia continues to enslave women; Taiwan has the highest per capita prostitution rate, while Japan has criminal syndicates kidnapping and trafficking women all over Asia. Thailand was the capital of sex trafficking until Cambodia gained that dubious distinction. *Why does Asia hate its women?*

Just as I was getting ready to shake my fist at God in anger, he reminded me that he weeps more for these women than I do. God weeps for these women, who are made in his image. He looks at each of them and sees a precious daughter. Where others see a prostitute, he sees his child. He wants to speak words of dignity and tell her that she's beloved. Others say "worthless," "useless," "less than," but he speaks the word *chosen*. She is chosen by him to steward the gift of being a woman and an Asian.

Jesus knows personally the pain of being judged, misunderstood, underestimated. He knows what it means to be shunned by others and have your body bought and sold. He knows the depth of the sorrow and the pain of the women in the red-light district of Bangkok. I could catch only a glimpse.

Embracing One's Gender and Ethnicity

That night, as I prayed for the women, I found myself blaming their ethnicity and their gender for their situations. The prostitution that I witnessed, the lack of options for Asian women, the attitudes of the community did not connect with what I thought was God's truth. Are they made in his image? Are they precious and chosen? Does God care about their situation? That night, God began to show me that he did not make a mistake—one ethnicity or gender is not better than another. He had chosen to make each of those women Thai and female. And in the same way, I was not a mistake. God chose to make me Japanese and female. The process of embracing my gender and my ethnicity began that night.

I had spent most of my academic life trying to overcome the perceived flaws of my gender and of my race. In class I would speak first and speak often. I played sports during free time—basketball, football, ultimate. I didn't want to be some Asian girl who was scared of being dirty. I loved the look of surprise from the guys on the field when they asked, "Do you play?"

Over the years I began to see how some "flaws" of my gender and race became God's tools for redemption. I hated my grandparents' refusal to tell me stories of what it was like to be Japanese American during World War II. But God returned that back to me as the gift of long-suffering. I hated the way my friends clumped together at social gatherings, so I asserted my independence. But God returned it to me as the gift of interdependence. I despised my programmed politeness that kept me from saying the angry words that boiled up within me. But God returned that to me as graciousness.

God reassured me that of all the ethnicities and genders he could have chosen for me, he chose Asian and female. He took my flaws and redeemed them to be used for his king-dom. My gender and ethnicity are God's gift to me—not an obstacle to overcome. These are my gifts to steward for others and for his kingdom.

Living in Tension

Asian Pacific Islander women live in tension. We live between "Asian" and "American," "woman" and "daughter." Society has strong scripts for people of different ethnicities. And within those scripts, Asian culture has expectations and socially ap-propriate roles. Navigating multiple worlds is an everyday re-ality for the authors of this book. Kathy was a successful jour-nalist who became a powerful manager in a nonprofit organization. But when she returns home, her father-in-law expects her to cut him fruit and make him a sandwich. I go from being a conference speaker one moment to being mis-taken for a college freshman the next. We may be women of impressive accomplishments, but we are regularly called "cute" and mistaken for teens because of our size.

The roads to being a woman, being Asian, being Ameri-can, being a Christian are each paved and well marked. But when they are combined, which road do we choose? Asian Pa-cific Islander women and our situations are as diverse as the many glorious body types that we come in. We want to share our stories of the ways that we've navigated the journey. We want to share our experiences, our struggles, our discoveries, in the hope of helping more women discover the truth about who God made them to be and how that can be used to ac-complish his purposes.

Expanding Gender Roles

Serving tea or chai is the women's role in many Asian Pacific Islander family circles. Often, young girls are taught the ritu-als. Stir the pot this way, hold your wrist just so, serve the most important guest first. The rituals pass down, from mother to daughter, secrets of the kitchen. Serving tea is a stereotype, but it also embodies great features of Asian culture—hospitality and service. Serving tea may be a simple act, but sometimes we are serving more than tea. At times, this cultural act is serving comfort, care or compassion to friends or family.

But Asian women are not limited to serving tea and sympathy. In this day of grande Tazo tea from Starbucks (two bags, please), women do more than serve tea. We serve our communities, our companies, our churches and our God. We want to embrace the positive attributes of Asian traditions and celebrate the gifts that culture brings to God's kingdom while letting go of the stereotypes that limit women to that role.

Biculturalism Leads to One Woman's Acceptance of Bisexuality

Beverly Yuen Thompson

Beverly Yuen Thompson earned a Ph.D. in sociology from the New School for Social Research and has taught at Florida International University.

Growing up Asian American has its own set of problems, but adding sexual identity issues to the equation forces one to be even more of an outsider. Searching for identity in a world in which most people are heterosexual and of homogenous ethnicity can be a daunting task and lead one to feel completely alone, like an "other" in the world. Fortunately, there are a growing number of hapa (biracial) support groups forming in the United States, including groups of those of alternative sexuality. Ultimately one must come to terms with one's ethnic and sexual identity and challenge racism, sexism, homophobia, and other prejudices with the help of those who are similarly challenged.

I had been wondering about taking part in a student theatre project about being Asian American, and I said to Tommy, "The thing is, I don't feel as though I've really lived the . . . Asian American experience." (Whatever I thought that was.)

Tommy kind of looked at me. And he said, "But, Claire, *you are* Asian American. So whatever experience you have lived, *that is* the Asian American experience."

I have never forgotten that.

> —*Claire Huang Kinsley,*
> *"Questions People Have Asked Me.*
> *Questions I Have Asked Myself"*

Claire Huang Kinsley articulates a common sentiment among multiracial Asian Americans regarding their racial and ethnic identity. She describes the reaction that her mixed heritage has provoked from Asians and Anglos, both of whom frequently view her as the "other." In response to these reactions, her faith in her racial identity has been shaken, and she feels unable to identify herself—fearful of being alienated for choosing either her Chinese or Anglo heritage, or both. Although she knows that she is mixed race, the question that still plagues her is whether or not she is included in the term "Asian American."

When I first read Kinsley's article, I was elated to find recognition of a biracial Asian American experience that resembled my own. I have a Chinese mother and an Anglo American father, as does she, and I am constantly confronted with questions about my ethnic background from curious individuals. Like Kinsley, I also question my ability to call myself Asian American because of my mixed heritage. However, in addition to my mixed heritage, I am also bisexual, which brings with it additional complications and permutations around my identity formation and self-understanding. The process of identity formation, especially of multiple identities, is complex and lifelong, and my experiences have been no exception.

Searching for an Identity

Though I have always understood that I was mixed race, a true understanding of what this meant in terms of my self-understanding and my relation to the dominant culture and Asian American communities did not develop until I was much older. My first exposure to the political side of identity politics came at the ages of fourteen and fifteen, when I began to develop a feminist understanding of the world around me. Then, at seventeen, I first began to call myself bisexual after two years of questioning my sexuality and believing that the only options that were available were either a lesbian or straight identity. Finally, at the age of nineteen I began to uncover the history of Asians in America through my college course work and developed a newfound understanding of my racial identity and its political implications. Yet, as is usually the case, this process was never as linear as it may sound.

Growing up, I was very aware that I was both Chinese and white—but I did not possess a term or racial category that recognized my position. Instead of creating or claiming a category that would accommodate me, I was left in confusion. How was it possible that I existed outside of the racial order of the census forms in my grade school, and what would I have to do in order to correctly fill in the answer to my racial puzzle? This confusion led to great discussions with my father about how I should identify myself. Well-meaning as he was, the only answer that he could arrive at was to choose between the two. This answer did not satisfy me because it would imply that I would be choosing between my parents—a choice I could not make.

Multiracials of Asian descent have a variety of choices available for self-identification; however, this "choice" may become obscured by others who may be quick to categorize based upon their own monoracial template of racial understanding. Physical traits are frequently scrutinized as ethnic signifiers, and one's mixed-race identity may not be accepted by outsiders. Maria P. P. Root elaborates: "To assume that the biracial person will racially identify with how they look is presumptive, but pervasive. Besides, the biracial person is perceived differently by different people. *Many persons make the mistake of thinking the biracial person is fortunate to have a choice; however, the reality is that the biracial person has to fight very hard to exercise choices that are not congruent with how they may be visually or emotionally perceived.*" Biracials and multiracials, then, develop a racial identity that risks criticism or denial from others; this influences the ways in which they self-identify, which may change in different contexts. When faced with the "What are you?" question, multiracials may try and consider what the person is really asking and respond accordingly. Racial fluidity is difficult to "see" in a world constructed by mutually exclusive categories based on a black–white dichotomy.

Problems Growing Up

When I was growing up in white-dominated Spokane, Washington, I spent most of my childhood, like most children, trying to fit in. My racial identity would raise its head occasionally, but most of the time I did not consider race. However, I did spend a great deal of energy rejecting my Chinese heritage, which I thought would certainly differentiate me from my white classmates. I would not allow my mother to teach me Chinese, which she attempted to do; I made fun of the Chinese food in the restaurants where she would take us; and I identified more and more with my father, whose side I would take when he belittled my mother's culture and "superstitions." I thought that if I did not speak Chinese then I could use that as proof that I really was white like everyone else. However, when we did end up in Seattle's Chinatown on vacation, I was secretly proud and impressed that my mother could speak in Chinese to the waitresses and would beg her to do so.

When my racial identity was used against me by my peers in school, it was an upsetting experience. One day in my grade school the other children began teasing me and a classmate, Michael, who was Chinese. Based on our racial similarities, they joked that we were dating. I was horrified to have my classmates group me with this Chinese boy. I took offense, and from that moment on I tried to distance myself from Michael. I thought that if I were friends with him then the Chinese in me would be brought to the surface—made more obvious—and that would be *the* reason we were friends. There were only three Asians in my grade school, and we were two of them; the only other was my best friend, Cassie, who was also *hapa*, or of mixed Asian/Pacific Islander descent. Cassie had a white mother and a Japanese father, who owned a Japanese restaurant downtown, and was therefore never around her house at the same time as any of her friends. She passed as white, and without her father around to connote her Japanese ancestry, her identity was never at issue. Curiously, never once in my eight-year friendship with her did we ever discuss our similar racial identities.

Discovering Feminism

When a few years later I began reading feminist books, I developed a feminist consciousness that consumed all aspects of my life. It fundamentally changed the way I understood myself and the world around me. I was ignited and passionate, seeking out feminist organizations where I could take part in concrete actions around my political philosophy. Yet the literature I read lacked a racial analysis, and this carried over into my developing consciousness. I had moved to Seattle to attend college, and I became active with the National Organization of Women (NOW), Clinic Defense Project, a youth socialist organization, and a queer youth group based in Spokane. I traveled between Seattle and Spokane a great deal and was politically active in both cities. I began to meet many people whose politics and sexual orientation were diverse, and I questioned my own long-held beliefs. My new roommate came out as a lesbian, and we learned a great deal about each other through that experience. She was also a hapa—mixed Hawaiian, Filipina, and white—and she would attempt to engage in racial identity conversations, but that topic did not hold me as much as discussions of politics and sexuality. I had begun to question my sexual orientation: I no longer proclaimed myself heterosexual, yet neither did I adopt a lesbian identity.

Finding a Sexual Identity

As I had years earlier agonized between the choice of seeing myself as Chinese or white, I now agonized between the choice of lesbian or straight. I knew that neither choice represented my feelings, yet I could not comprehend another option. The messages that I received from both the lesbian community and dominant straight society was the same: choose. When I was in college, at around the age of seventeen, I realized that bisexuality existed as an option, and immediately I knew that was the identity that most accurately described who I felt I was. But I also knew that claiming a bisexual identity would be a hardship because others would analyze me through their monosexual template of understanding. Indeed I ran across many people who demanded to know, "Which do you *really* like better, boys or girls?" This question reminded me of how my ethnic identity had often elicited the query, "What are you?" People were again confused. Now both my racial and sexual identity crossed lines of demarcation, enacting border-crossings that people have assumed are unnatural and problematic.

Root suggests that the "racially mixed woman may be more open to exploring sexual orientation" because of their lived experience of understanding racial identity as complex. Therefore, this understanding of racial identity may "transfer over to viewing sexual orientation as flexible and sexual identity as *mutable*." Throughout my life I have had to explain my racial identity instead of having an easy and ready-made label like most monoracials. Yet, besides the occasional difficulty of explaining my race, I also enjoyed being more than one, having more options, and enjoying the benefit of traveling in more than one group. Now with my emerging sexuality, bisexuality seemed the natural conclusion. Already I was racially mixed and therefore I could understand the meaning of a bisexual identity in my own life. Somehow it all came together in a complementary fashion.

After I had come out as bisexual I began to embrace my Asian heritage and accept it back into my life. I was in my senior year at Eastern Washington University, and I began to focus my research on Asian American women and their history. Yet it was not until I went to graduate school in women's studies at San Diego State University that I gained greater exposure to Asian American culture and history. It was an awakening that I compare to the development of my feminist consciousness. I was both excited to find the material and angered that it had taken so long to discover Asian American history. I wrote on the Japanese internment, studied Chinese American history, and read every Asian American studies book I could find.

Slowly I discovered that, although I could relate to some of the issues and material, my reality as a young bisexual hapa woman was not being addressed. I began to question the place of the multiracial Asian in the academic fields of ethnic studies and women's studies. Ethnic studies seemed to focus overwhelmingly on families that fit a specific model—namely, a heterosexual family made up of two immigrant parents of the same ethnicity and the conflicts their children face negotiating between their Asian parents and Anglo society. In women's studies, there was an awareness and commentary on race and difference among women, but that usually focused on the black—white racial dichotomy; Asian American women were rarely mentioned. Where was I to find myself represented in academic theory that claimed to represent women and racial minorities? As I studied further, however, I became aware that I was not the only one grappling with these issues: there were hapa groups forming around the country as well as magazines and books that were addressing this issue and demanding acceptance within the Asian American community and academy.

My challenge in graduate school, as I saw it, was to explore where I could find myself reflected, with all my complexity, in the literature of ethnic studies and women's studies.

Comedienne Margaret Cho, performing during the 2007 True Colors tour supporting gay rights. Cho is both Asian American and bisexual. AP Images.

As Dana Y. Takagi suggests, it is crucial to recognize "different sexual practices and identities that also claim the label Asian American" in order to begin to challenge notions of identity that have, in the past, been accepted "unproblematically and uncritically in Asian American Studies." Within the "Asian American experience" there is a great deal of diversity that has thus far remained underexplored. Issues of interracial relationships, transracial adoption, biracial identity, and queer identity have remained marginalized and considered exceptions to an unspoken norm of Asian American identity. David Eng and Alice Hom believe it is imperative "to recognize that Asian Americans are never purely, or merely, racial subjects" and to dissolve any rigid or monolithic definitions. Once monolithic norms are instituted, diversity and complexity are shut out and remain excluded.

Feeling Alone

I have seen these norms instituted in a variety of ways within identity base groups in my experiences. Organizations and literature on identity deemphasize aspects that are not considered directly related to the main unifying force they address. I have found myself continuing this silence when in group situations because of the offhanded manner in which comments regarding these other aspects are received. For example, I have usually found myself to be the only Asian American in queer organizations; therefore I feel uncomfortable bringing attention to racial issues because this would presumably turn me into both an object of curiosity and an educator. I prefer to discuss racial issues with others who have similar experiences so that we can share on an equal basis and validate each other in respectful and mutual ways. At the same time, when I am in organizations that focus on racial identity, I also feel silence around sexual identity because, again, I do not want to position myself as an object or educator. In other words, I do not want to detract from my connection with others. Unfortunately, connection is usually based on one issue, with other aspects of identity being minimized instead of validated.

Segregating multiple identities in theories of race and gender results in fracturing self-understanding—separating one's gender from race and sexuality. This segregation is also an impossibility: at any moment we inhabit all of our identities and may face discrimination on any or all levels. It is a painful experience to seek out a community based on race, gender, or sexuality only to have other identities denied and rejected. As Karen Maeda Allman reasons, "Mixed-race lesbians may be suspicious of any kind of identity politics based on single-group membership, whether based on race, gender, or sexual orientation. Too many opportunities exist to exclude us, to declare us as suspect *others*." When people of color come out as queer, race is an important consideration. Rejection from one's racial/ethnic community based on homophobia, and from the queer community based on racism, is a very real consequence that may bar individuals from true acceptance in any specific community. As a hapa bisexual, I am constantly seeking out inclusion and acceptance of my sexuality in the Asian American community as well as acceptance of my racial identity in the bisexual and queer community.

Finding Others Like Herself

Paula C. Rust comments that "a positive integration of one's racial, ethnic, or class identity with one's sexual identity is greatly facilitated by support from others who share an individual's particular constellation of identities." The first time I experienced being around others with my "constellation of identities" was when I attended the second national conference of the Asian and Pacific-Islander Lesbian and Bisexual Women's Network at UCLA in July of 1998. One of the workshops at this conference was titled "Mixed Girls in the Mix: Hapas, Mixed Breeds, and Other Racial Misfits." Attending this session was a homecoming for me. Never before had I sat in a room filled with hapas who were both bisexual and lesbian. Of the twenty-plus attendees at the workshop, there was a vast array of racial and ethnic diversity. Half of the women were Asian and white, while the other half of the room represented a great diversity of mixed-race hapa women. We explored and discussed numerous issues, and for many of us it was an amazing and eye-opening experience merely to be around other women with whom we had so much in common—and yet still so much in difference. The workshop went overtime, making it very evident that this group needed more time together. Therefore the group decided to create a hapa caucus. Later that evening when the caucuses met, some of the women chose to go to the caucus groups of their ethnicities and some returned to the hapa caucus; we again had to choose between identifying as hapa over our monoethnic options.

I met several women in this newly formed caucus who also identified as both biracial and bisexual. When I mentioned that I was doing research on biracial and bisexual Asian women, one of the women exclaimed, "The bi-bi girls!" and went on to explain that she herself was a "bi-bi girl" as were some of her friends. I was overflowing with excitement to meet someone who shared my same "constellation of identities" and had even coined a term for this identity.

Straddling Categories

Rust speaks to this topic of the "bi-bi" identity: "Many bisexuals of mixed race or ethnicity feel a comfortable resonance between their mixed heritage and their bisexuality. In a society where both racial-ethnic and sexual categories are highly elaborated, individuals of mixed heritage or who are bisexual find themselves straddling categories that are socially constructed as distinct from one another." Rust captures the ideological and theoretical similarities of bisexual and multiracial identities in this passage, echoing my own experiences of these two identities. Because of the exclusion bisexuals and biracials experience in monoracial and monosexual communities, different responses result when these mixed identities come together in the same individual. For some, this combination brings a sense of familiarity, of being once again outside of the box, of confusing people. Others, however, may be disappointed that they are again marginalized, unwilling to deal with further oppression.

When I think that I must choose between another set of boxes—straight or lesbian—I feel the same pressure and the same inability as I felt choosing between white and Chinese, between my mother and my father. My choice was made for me. It was written on my skin; my face and gestures reflect both parents who made me. And the choice of who I love is decided for me: I love both my mother and my father and will never deny love and acceptance for someone based on their gender or race. Marian M. Sciachitano believes that "taking up a bicultural and biracial politics of difference" means accepting "the contradictions, the uneasiness, and the ambiguity" of such an identity, which may also apply to a bisexual label and the interaction of the two. Yet the contradictions, uneasiness, and ambiguity are imposed from the outside and arise when I must fit myself into the established mutually exclusive order. For myself, I find comfort in the middle ground, in the ability to transgress and question lines of demarcation and challenge systematic segregation.

Challenging Stereotypes and the Status Quo

I am hapa because I am the descendent of two cultures, two languages, and two people who came together across these boundaries. I am firmly located in the late twentieth century in the United States, where interracial marriages have only been legal for a generation. I am one of many people who are hapa, Amerasian, mixed breeds, and mutts. I am constantly called Japanese, Korean, Chinese, Oriental. I am comfortable in other people's discomfort. I am hurt that I denied my mother a proper place in my life. She has divorced my father and has gone to live with Chinese female friends from her childhood, her other life within which I will never be truly included. When I visit her I am left out of the conversation, but the sound of Cantonese soothes me. Sometimes when I pay attention I realize that I am able to follow their body language and remember some Chinese words, but it is the English phrases that are a part of their Chinese American vocabulary that always give me the final gist. I am loyal to my Chinese heritage, I am loyal to my white heritage, and I am loyal to my antiracist beliefs.

I am bisexual because I recognize that both women and men have contributed to my life and I want the freedom to choose a partner based on a person's integrity rather than on genitalia. I am firmly located not only in a time when queer people are oppressed but also in a time when a vital queer community has developed that gives me the ability to understand what that identity means. I am one of many people who are bisexual, queer, fence sitters, and switch hitters. I am called queer, dyke, straight. I am comfortable in other people's discomfort. I am loyal to my love for women, I am loyal to my love for men, and I am loyal to my beliefs in feminism and antiheterosexism.

The question that still lingers in my mind is who will be loyal to me? Which group/community/movement(s) will claim me as their member and comrade? I want to see a movement against oppression that does not trivialize or deny me any aspect of my identity, that recognizes the interconnectedness of my sexuality, race, gender, and politics. I am one of many people whose fight against oppression does not end with their gender, race, or sexuality alone. I am reminded of the words of Teresa Kay Williams; "One day, the debate on passing will become obsolete (will pass), when Asian-descent multiracials can express the full range of their humanity in which boundaries of race, ethnicity, nation, class, gender, sexuality, body, and language can be crossed and transgressed without judgement, without scorn, and without detriment." I find a great deal of comfort reading these words by authors whose identities are similar to my own. I know that I am not alone in this world that consistently tries to deny the existence of multiracials and bisexuals. Merely by existing I am challenging stereotypes and the status quo. This battle against racism, sexism, and bi/homophobia is being fought on many fronts by people who are like me, people who have my back.

Asian Women Are Still Not Completely Accepted in the United States

Iris Chang

Iris Chang is the author of The Rape of Nanking, Thread of the Silkworm, *and* The Chinese in America: A Narrative History, *from which this excerpt is taken.*

Asian Americans live to attain the same American dream as any other Americans. Without their contributions, America would not be the same country it is today. Despite the remarkable success of many Asian American women, full acceptance into mainstream American society is slow in coming. Such notable Asian American women as television personality Connie Chung, architect Maya Lin, novelist Amy Tan, and skater Michelle Kwan have been victimized by the prejudice of mainstream Americans.

From the moment the Chinese set foot on American soil, their dreams have been American dreams. They scrambled for gold in the dirt of California. They aspired to own their own land and businesses, and fought to have their children educated in American schools alongside other American children. Like most immigrant groups, they came here fleeing war and famine, persecution and poverty. And like the descendants of other immigrant groups, their children have come to call the United States home.

The America of today would not be the same America without the achievements of its ethnic Chinese. Generation after generation, they worked to build the American nation to its present level of greatness. Some fought in the Civil War and built the railroad that welded the country together. Their early struggles for justice created new foundations of law later used by the civil rights movement. They built America's earliest rockets and helped win the cold war. In Silicon Valley and elsewhere, their contributions helped establish and maintain U.S. supremacy in the information age. Today, they are dispersed in every profession imaginable: as inventors, teachers, authors, doctors, engineers, lawyers, CEOs, social workers, accountants, architects, police chiefs, firefighters, actors, and astronauts.

But sadly, despite this long legacy of contribution, many Chinese Americans continue to be regarded as foreigners. "Go back where you came from" is a taunt most new immigrants have faced at some point. As one put it, "Asian Americans feel like we're a guest in someone else's house, that we can never really relax and put our feet up on the table." Accents and cultural traditions may disappear, but skin tone and the shape of one's eyes do not. These features have eased the way for some to regard ethnic Chinese people as exotic and different—certainly not "real" Americans. Thus the Americanization of Chinese Americans has been overshadowed by the convenient but dishonest stereotypes in the mass market, which portray them as innately and irreversibly different from their fellow Americans.

What, in human terms, is the impact of such divisiveness? It's a native-born Californian, a West Covina city council member, being told over the phone, "Funny, you don't sound like a Wong. You sound so *American*." It's the virtual absence of Chinese American doctors on medical TV dramas, when in actuality one in every six medical doctors in the United States is Asian American. It's a famous Chinese American movie star with good reviews in serious work reporting that she and her colleagues are always asked by studios to "don our accents and use our high kicks à la Jackie Chan or a Bond girl." It's the decision of the Mattel toy company not to release an Asian Barbie doll in their year 2000 fantasy collection of future female American presidents, even though white, black, and Hispanic dolls are included. ("People like Asian-American dolls in costumes, not as president," notes Berkeley professor Elaine Kim. "This tells us how we are thought of.") . . .

Scratch the surface of every American celebrity of Chinese heritage and you will find that, no matter how stellar their achievements, no matter how great their contribution to U.S. society, virtually all of them have had their identities questioned at one point or another.

Connie Chung, the second woman in American history to co-anchor a network nightly news broadcast, survived an unwelcoming newsroom atmosphere. Being one of the few women was bad enough, but as she adds, "In those early days at CBS, '71 to '76, people were saying 'Yellow Journalism'— little remarks that were clearly racist." But as late as 1990, Cliff Kincaid, a radio host in Washington, D.C., would call her "Connie Chink."

Maya Lin, now the most famous female architect in the United States, was viciously attacked when, as a Yale undergraduate in 1980, she won a nationwide contest to design the Vietnam Veterans Memorial in Washington, D.C. "How can you let a gook design this?" some veterans asked. "How did it happen that an Asian-American woman was permitted to make a memorial for American men who died fighting in Asia?"

After her novel *The Joy Luck Club* became a literary blockbuster, author Amy Tan had to struggle to get it produced in Hollywood. Before the movie was released, one film executive complained to Chris Lee, the Chinese American president of Columbia TriStar, that there were "no Americans" in *The Joy Luck Club.* Lee retorted, "There are Americans in it. They just don't look like you."

At the 1998 Olympics, when U.S. figure skater Michelle Kwan finished second after her teammate Tara Lipinski, the headlines on MSNBC read, "American beats Kwan." Many Chinese Americans were distressed that the media automatically considered Kwan a foreigner when in fact she had been born, reared, and trained in the United States. Four years later, this error was repeated after Kwan lost the gold medal to Sarah Hughes. In a secondary headline, the *Seattle Times* announced, "American outshines Kwan, Slutskaya in skating surprise."

In 2001, Elaine Chao, a Harvard Business School graduate who had served as chairman of the Federal Maritime Commission and assistant secretary of transportation, made history as the first Chinese American to accept a Cabinet position when President George W. Bush named her secretary of labor. When her critics attacked her business ties with China, her husband, Senator Mitch McConnell (R-Ky.) saw "subtle racism," "yellow fever," and xenophobic attitudes in the media.

Time and again, the question is posed within the Chinese American community: How many hoops do we have to jump through to be considered "real" Americans?

More Women Are Working, But Job Equality Remains Elusive

International Labour Organization (ILO)

The International Labour Organization (ILO) is a United Nations agency that brings together governments, employers and workers of its member states in common action to promote decent work throughout the world.

While more women are working worldwide than ever before, serious disparities remain between women and men in the workplace. Throughout most of the world, unemployment for women remains substantially higher than for men. And many women who do find jobs comprise the large quantity of working poor, those whose incomes cannot sustain a family. The so-called glass ceiling, which limits the prestige and income for working women, is still firmly in place. Yet societal views are slowly changing with regard to women in the workplace, as employers begin to realize that valuing their female employees leads to benefits for all.

GENEVA (ILO News)—Women are entering the global labour force in record numbers, but they still face higher unemployment rates and lower wages and represent 60 per cent of the world's 550 million working poor, says a new report by the International Labour Office (ILO) prepared for International Women's Day.

At the same time, a separate updated analysis of trends in the efforts of women to break through the glass ceiling says the rate of success in crashing through the invisible, symbolic barrier to top managerial jobs remains "slow, uneven and sometimes discouraging".

"These two reports provide a stark picture of the status of women in the world of work today", says ILO Director-General Juan Somavia. "Women must have an equal chance of reaching the top of the jobs ladder. And, unless progress is made in taking women out of poverty by creating productive and decent employment, the Millennium Development Goals of halving poverty by 2015 will remain out of reach in most regions of the world."

"Global Employment Trends for Women 2004", an analysis of female employment, says more women work today than ever before. In 2003, 1.1 billion of the world's 2.8 billion workers, or 40 per cent, were women, representing a worldwide increase of nearly 200 million women in employment in the past 10 years.

Still, the explosive growth in the female workforce hasn't been accompanied by true socio-economic empowerment for women, the report said. Nor has it led to equal pay for work of equal value or balanced benefits that would make women equal to men across nearly all occupations. "In short, true equality in the world of work is still out of reach," the report adds.

The study found that while the gap between the number of men and women in the labour force (the sum of the unemployed and employed) has been decreasing in all regions of the world since 1993, this decrease has varied widely. While women in the transition economies and East Asia—where the number of women working per 100 men is 91 and 83 respectively—have nearly closed the gap, in other regions of the world such as the Middle East, North Africa and South Asia, only 40 women per 100 men are economically active, the report says.

Meanwhile, female unemployment in 2003 was slightly higher than male unemployment for the world as a whole (6.4 per cent for female, 6.1 per cent for male), the ILO said, leaving 77.8 million women who were willing to work and looking for work without employment. Only in East Asia and sub-Saharan Africa did the regional male unemployment rate exceed that of women, with 3.7 per cent male unemployment in East Asia compared to 2.7 per cent female unemployment, and 11.8 per cent unemployment for men in sub-Saharan Africa compared to 9.6 per cent female unemployment.

In Latin America and the Caribbean, the female unemployment rate was 10.1 per cent compared to the male rate of 6.7 per cent, while in the Middle East and North Africa the female unemployment rate of 16.5 per cent was 6 percentage points higher than that of men. For young people in general, but specifically for young women aged 15 to 24 years, the difficulty in finding work was even more drastic, with 35.8 million young women involuntarily unemployed worldwide.

In developing countries, women simply cannot afford to not work, the report says, noting that low unemployment rates thus mask the problem. The challenge for women in these countries is not gaining employment—they have to take whatever work is available and are likely to wind up in informal sector work such as agriculture with little, if any, social security benefits and a high degree of vulnerability—but in gaining decent and productive employment, the report says.

What's more, of the world's 550 million working poor—or persons unable to lift themselves and their families above the USD 1 per day threshold—330 million, or 60 per cent, are women, the report says. Adding the 330 million female working poor to the 77.8 million women who are unemployed means that at least 400 million decent jobs would be needed to provide unemployed and working poor women with a way out of poverty.

"Unless progress is made to take women out of working poverty by creating employment opportunities to help them secure productive and remunerative work in conditions of freedom, security and human dignity and thereby giving women the chance to work themselves out of poverty, the Millennium Development Goal of halving poverty by 2015 will not be reached in most regions of the world", the report says.

The report also found that women typically earn less than men. In the six occupations studied, women still earn less of what their male co-workers earn, even in "typically female" occupations such as nursing and teaching.

"Creating enough decent jobs for women is only possible if policy makers place employment at the centre of social and economic polices and recognize that women face more substantial challenges in the workplace than men", Mr. Somavia says. "Raising incomes and opportunities for women lifts whole families out of poverty and it drives economic and social progress."

The Glass Ceiling Is Still Intact

"Recent global statistics show that women continue to increase their share of managerial positions, but the rate of progress is slow, uneven and sometimes discouraging", says "Breaking through the glass ceiling: Women in management—Update 2004."

The overall employment situation for women hasn't evolved significantly since 2001, the update says. Women's share of professional jobs increased by just 0.7 per cent between 1996 and 1999, and 2000 and 2002. And with women's share of managerial positions in some 60 countries ranging between 20 and 40 per cent, the data show that women are markedly under-represented in management compared to their overall share of employment.

In politics, the proportion of women representatives in national parliaments remains low, increasing from 13 per cent to 15.2 per cent between 1999 and 2003. However, the update did find recent increases in the number of women in traditionally male-dominated cabinet posts, such as foreign affairs, finance and defence.

Women's overall share of professional jobs in 2000–2002 was highest in Eastern Europe and the Commonwealth of Independent States (CIS), largely due to long-standing policies supporting working mothers. Women's share of professional jobs in South Asian and Middle Eastern countries was markedly lower at around 30 per cent or less, due, the report says, to societal views of women's labour force participation and to women prioritising family responsibilities.

Data show that, in general, countries in North America, South America and Eastern Europe have a higher share of women in management jobs than countries in East Asia, South Asia and the Middle East. Nevertheless, the report indicates, "in female-dominated sectors where there are more women managers, a disproportionate number of men rise to the more senior positions and in those professions normally reserved for men, women managers are few and far between".

One exception was the high incidence of women holding top jobs in legal systems in some countries. In 2001–2002, more than 50 per cent of the judges in six Eastern European countries (Hungary, Romania, the Czech Republic and Estonia, Croatia and Lithuania) and 35 per cent of the highest judges in Poland were women. And in early 2003, out of the 18 judges elected to the International Criminal Court (ICC), 10 were women.

Says the ILO's Linda Wirth, Director of the ILO Gender Bureau and author of the original study: "Women continue to have more difficulty obtaining top jobs than they do lower down the hierarchy. A handful of women are making headlines here and there as they break through, but statistically they represent a mere few per cent of top management jobs. The rule of thumb is still: the higher up an organisation's hierarchy, the fewer the women."

Yet the news isn't all bad. The study says some employers are beginning to shift attitudes and businesses now understand that family-friendly policies, improved access to training, and stronger mentoring systems encourage female staff retention and can improve productivity. And governments and unions are advocating the reform of employment and welfare legislation to ensure that mothers can maintain seniority, benefits, and earning potential.

Feminism Is Not Dead, Just Evolving

Eleanor Holmes Norton

Eleanor Holmes Norton has served as a congresswoman in the United States House of Representatives. She was chosen by President Jimmy Carter to be the first woman chair of the Equal Employment Opportunity Commission. She has also been a civil rights movement leader, a feminist leader, a professor of law at Georgetown University, and a board member of three Fortune 500 companies.

The feminist revolution changed life in America and the world. Today's young women, who may not consider themselves feminists, are the beneficiaries of everything that their pioneering mothers did to change the dynamics between men and women. But there are still reactionaries who seek to reerect the walls that kept women subservient for so many years. These backward-looking people believe that just because the active revolution has subsided, women are not as interested in feminism anymore. But they are wrong. Feminism has not died, just matured and progressed. The movement is still on course.

I am not everywoman, especially considering that I am a black woman. I am, however, many women of every background and color who crossed into forbidden territory to begin the modern feminist movement in the 1960s. Nearly forty years later, women are not what they were. Even the bit parts I have played tell much about how the great feminist awakening opened a new world for women: law student, activist in the then-new Civil Rights and Feminist Movements, constitutional lawyer, professor of law, local public official, chair of the U.S. Equal Employment Opportunity Commission, member of Congress. At the same time, of course, most of us also were intent on playing the irresistible roles in which women had always been cast. Like most, I was a wife. I am a mother. Very little of the rest of what we have done with our lives was possible for our mothers. Young and daring, we were the first women in any numbers who insisted that we were entitled to try for it all. We did it, running all the way, sometimes stumbling or falling down, yet running still.

Breaking Down the Wall

No one can doubt that we have shaken to its foundation the great wall that the ages have built around women. This wall, the oldest in human time, had been impenetrable for most women, and invisible to many. For all its different manifestations, the wall has had similar effects on women living in vastly different societies throughout the world. The origins are elusive. In the beginning, men everywhere probably used their physical strength to claim and enforce dominance when physicality was what mattered most for survival. Once male dominance was achieved physically, the rest was not difficult to maintain—until now.

We were not the first women who sought to be as free as men. We were the first who brought a combination of insistence and tactics fit for a wall that stood on the firmest foundation. Our insistence, of course, was aided and abetted by forces larger than our will. Our society had finally achieved control over certain forces that had controlled people in all societies, especially women—ranging from the consequences of fertility, childbirth, and children to changes in the economy and in the nature of work.

My generation's insight was that finally the proverbial wall that divided the sexes, enforcing male superiority in human endeavors, could be taken down. Like all great insights, this one drew its power from the refusal to allow distraction from a potent idea. We demurred to the argument that the wall sometimes had the appearance—and for some women, even the characteristics—of a protective shield. Our goal was to make a revolution, and revolutions are not made by yielding to distractions. A generation later, as we carry forward a revolution that cannot be contained, the complexity of the feminist quest is more easily acknowledged. Today we confront the consequences of the extraordinary changes we have made. Inevitably, the progress that has transformed the lives of millions of American women also has been accompanied by its share of confusion and opposition. Moreover, as it developed, feminism itself helped foster new challenges. New insights are necessary to help meet new issues facing a new generation of women.

Opposition to Feminism

The kaleidoscopic quality of the wall that both denied and protected women helps to explain why we were the first generation to insist that the wall, all of it, should come down—and also explains why we are still going at it, and why the generations after us sometimes appear less intense about the feminist mission. Not surprisingly, there are efforts to fortify the wall in the name of marriage, children, and family. Such attempts have some currency because unlike other "inferior" beings, women have always had a uniquely intimate relationship with the men who claimed superiority and dominion over them. This bond remains one of the great mysteries of life. Happily, love and sex always survive revolutions. We wanted women to have more of both. It is no accident that the sexual revolution and the feminist revolution began at the same time or that such profound departures would draw strong reactions. The inevitable questions have been raised. Foremost among them, of course, is how much can the wall be challenged without endangering one of the closest and most important relationships in human existence? Feminists of my generation believe this was a false challenge, then as now. In the process of bringing down the wall, however, such questions cannot simply be shunted aside. They help explain much about the difference between the era of those who made the revolution and the period of those who have inherited it.

The relationship between men and women also casts light on why the subordination of women in the relationship was not systematically challenged earlier. The complicated bond between men and women—one of the permanent wonders of the world—always asserts itself and often obscures the structural defects in the wall. Patriarchy gets confused with fatherhood, manliness with male supremacy. But it is male bias we are after, not males. Without feminist consciousness, this confusion can overwhelm the separation between sex and sexism that my generation finally exposed.

The Women's Movement is not the first to be threatened by the resurgence of an old order. The difference is in the difficulty that comes from banishing part of the unique relationship between the sexes, clinging to the rest, and distinguishing between the two. Should the goal now be to plow ahead against the mountain of remaining gender bias or to concentrate on family, marriage, love, and sex? Have we come this far only to have our choices come down to these?

Catalytic Versus Functional Feminists

My generation walked up to the wall and saw unadulterated, unconquered gender bias for what it was. The new generation in the United States sees less of it because we have eliminated much of it. The difference between our generation and our daughters' is less important than it may seem, because the daughters grew up in a world where feminist aspirations were accepted as the way the world operates. That some women have not embraced what we call feminism or do not use the feminist label has had no effect on the pace of feminist change.

We were *catalytic feminists*. Younger women are *functional feminists*. The new generation has taken up our issues, changing the world more than we dared, opening many more doors for women, and making demands that did not cross our minds. Their remarkable pluralism defies one language, even the explicit language of feminism. Like every revolutionary vanguard, we were a smaller, more cohesive and homogeneous group. We needed to speak the language of feminism to be understood and to spread the revolution. The new generation says it in many ways, and moves still more women to feminist ideas and feminist modes.

The proof lies not in what they say but in how they act. Today's women think nothing of working on factory floors, driving buses, or building things. They believe it is their prerogative to walk into law firms, corporate boardrooms, surgical operating rooms, congressional hearing rooms, and presidential cabinet rooms. They thrill crowds who have never seen women as players in major sports until now. They have raised the quality of recruits in the armed services, who then rise through the ranks and serve in posts formerly reserved for men only. They do not hesitate to vote their issues as women. They are forging new personal and equal relationships with men.

Even traditional women and families act on a revised view of who a woman is. The average American may not call herself a feminist, yet the substance of the feminist revolution is a potent guide to the way she lives her life. The housewife lifestyle that defined a norm for many women when Betty Friedan wrote *The Feminine Mystique* is no more. The average woman is in the labor force. There is mass approval for work, even for women with young children, and even without universal, educational childcare—an urgent necessity that the new generation must win. Contraception, forbidden to be discussed or supported by government until feminists won that vital victory, is no longer controversial; abortion, one of the

Representative Eleanor Holmes Norton of Washington, DC, (right) stands next to Senator Hillary Clinton of New York at a 2001 rally calling for stronger enforcement of the Equal Pay Act. Alex Wong/Getty Images.

most important and controversial feminist goals, has the support of an American majority. Segregated education and sports, among the most entrenched of gender traditions, have met their match in federal law. These monumental barriers that helped solidify the wall throughout human history have fallen away in our country—but it's not over yet. The feminist revolution grows and spreads as women here, and in every corner of the earth, pursue their own versions of feminist progress.

Changing the Entire World

In spite of manifest changes, there are some who look past the enlargement of rights, the personal egalitarianism emerging between men and women, and the relaxation of resistance to feminist goals. Despite a new, assertive generation of our descendants, some skeptics fail to recognize the feminism of this generation because the daughters are not carbon copies of their mothers. In the reaction to feminism, many see the "end of feminism."

I do not underestimate the reactionaries, or the pressure on young women to revert to old traditions. There is much to learn, from the fight for women's suffrage in particular. That struggle took longer and was more laborious than ours has been in achieving far more for women. Suffrage released feminist ideas and changes beyond the vote, but that single-minded quest did not bequeath wholesale societal changes similar to those we see today. The reasons are complicated. However, it is clear that the sustained focus that proved necessary to achieve the vote ceased germinating other issues once that great victory was finally achieved. In contrast, the modern feminist agenda was crowded from the outset, and new issues have only multiplied. The work of feminism goes on, with countless women and men, consciously and not, moving it forward. Beyond our own country, the global spread of feminism and the changes pressed by the transformation of women have become an irreversible force that is changing the entire world.

An Unfinished Revolution

As my generation continues to struggle in our way, the new generation is finding its own way. Our "vanguard generation," of course, could become so intoxicated by the certainty that we have made history that it would be too easy to regard those who follow as insufficiently attentive to the revolution. But the descendants do not need to make the revolution; they are its first beneficiaries. The work of a new generation is both the same and different. It is the same to the extent that our revolution is unfinished. Yet it also is as different as today is from yesterday. To live, a revolution must build on the past, not relive it.

My generation cannot afford to become infatuated with the progress of the last forty years. We need only be confident that women cannot be turned back. Still, it is one thing to believe that our progress will continue; it is another to think that feminist advances are inevitable. To ask men to move over is to ask them to give up a monopoly on everything— power, jobs, athletics, and primacy in the family. Even so, the pace we set yesterday has only quickened.

There are two possible courses for great movements. They fire up, blaze, bring change, glow down into embers, and die—or they mature and keep growing.

Look around. Women are on course.

For Further Discussion

1. *The Joy Luck Club* is set in a period of women's rights, women's liberation, and feminist ideas that were breaking out in the United States in the 1960s and afterward. How is the book a reflection of the ideas voiced in chapter three, such as those by Toyama and Norton?

2. Though Suyuan Woo is dead before *The Joy Luck Club* begins, her past and her continuing presence hover over the book. How is she still an important figure in the story? (See Ho, Shen, Grice, Braendlin, and Chu.)

3. The depictions of men in *The Joy Luck Club* tend to be limited or negative. The husbands are shallow and demanding, and the fathers, in the words of one critic, "are distant and silent" (Elaine H. Kim). Why is this? Is this narrow portrait of men a strength or weakness of the book?

4. Many critics of *The Joy Luck Club* focus their discussion on the younger generation's attempt to carve out an identity for themselves. Are the daughters ever able to fully find themselves? Which daughters are the most successful at this? (See Ho, Shen, Grice, and Braendlin.)

5. Does the ending of *The Joy Luck Club* work in melding the needs of the older generation of mothers and the younger generation of daughters? Does it bring the closure and satisfaction that are characteristic of a successful ending? (See Braendlin, Chu, and Bow.)

6. Critics have found numerous similarities between Tan's life and the stories in *The Joy Luck Club*. Tan, conversely, has argued that there is little actual autobiography, and

that the book is merely an artistic rendering of reality. Which argument do you find more convincing, given the facts of Tan's own life as depicted in the articles in chapter one? (See Champion, Ling, and Tan.)

For Further Reading

Julia Alvarez   *How the Garcia Girls Lost Their Accents.* New York: Plume, 1992.

Sandra Cisneros   *The House on Mango Street.* New York: Random House, 1994.

Maxine Hong Kingston   *The Woman Warrior.* New York: Vintage, 1975.

Terri McMillan   *Waiting to Exhale.* New York: Viking, 1992.

Gloria Naylor   *The Women of Brewster Place.* New York: Penguin USA, 1982.

Lisa See   *Snow Flower and the Secret Fan.* New York: Random House, 2005.

Amy Tan   *The Kitchen God's Wife.* New York: G.P. Putnam's Sons, 1991.

Amy Tan   *The Hundred Secret Senses.* New York: G.P. Putnam's Sons, 1995.

Amy Tan   *The Bonesetter's Daughter.* New York: G.P. Putnum's Sons, 2001.

Amy Tan   *The Opposite of Fate: A Book of Musings.* New York: G.P. Putnum's Sons, 2003.

Bibliography

Books

Jennifer Baumgardner and Amy Richards	*Grassroots: A Field Guide for Feminist Activism.* New York: Farrar, Straus and Giroux, 2005.
Harold Bloom	*Amy Tan* (Modern Critical Views). Philadelphia: Chelsea House Publishers, 2000.
Ellen Bravo	*Taking on the Big Boys, or, Why Feminism Is Good for Families, Business, and the Nation.* New York: Feminist Press at the City University of New York, 2007.
Gayle Collins	*America's Women.* New York: William Morrow, 2003.
Cathy N. Davidson, Linda Wagner-Martin, and Elizabeth Ammons	*The Oxford Companion to Women's Writing in the United States.* New York: Oxford University Press, 1995.
SuEllen Hamkins and Renee Schultz	*The Mother-Daughter Project: How Mothers and Daughters Can Band Together, Beat the Odds, and Thrive Through Adolescence.* New York: Hudson Street Press, 2007.
J. Hannan	*Feminism.* Harlow, England: Pearson, 2007.

Elaine H. Kim   *Asian American Literature: An Introduction to the Writings and Their So-
cial Context.* Philadelphia: Temple
University Press, 1982.

Magali Cornier   *Feminism and the Postmodern Im-
Michael   pulse: Post-World War II Fiction.* Al-
bany: State University of New York
Press, 1996.

Magali Cornier   *New Visions of Community in Con-
Michael   temporary American Fiction: Tan,
Kingsolver, Castillo, Morrison.* Iowa
City: University of Iowa Press, 2006.

Sau-ling Cynthia   *Reading Asian American Literature:
Wong   From Necessity to Extravagance.* Princeton, New Jersey: Princeton University Press, 1993.

Periodicals

Patricia Hamilton   "Feng Shui, Astrology, and the Five
Elements: Traditional Chinese Belief
in *The Joy Luck Club.*" *MELUS*, Vol.
24, No. 2 (Summer 1999): 125–145.

Marina Heung   "'Such Opposite Creatures': Men and
Women in Asian American Litera-
ture." *Michigan Quarterly Review*, Vol.
29, No. 1 (Winter 1990): 68–93.

Marina Heung   "Daughter-text/Mother-text in Amy
Tan's *Joy Luck Club.*" *Feminist Studies*,
Vol. 19 (Fall 1993): 597–616.

P. Hunter   "Mother's Nature," *O, The Oprah
Magazine*, Vol. 8 No. 5 (May 2007):
283.

Melanie McAlister   "(Mis)Reading *The Joy Luck Club.*" *Asian America: Journal of Culture and the Arts*, Vol. 1 (1992): 102–18.

Malini Johar Schueller   "Theorizing Ethnicity and Subjectivity: Maxine Hong Kingston's *Tripmaster Monkey* and Amy Tan's *The Joy Luck Club.*" *Genders*, Vol. 15 (Winter 1992): 72–85.

Stephen Souris   "'Only Two Kinds of Daughters': Inter-monologue Dialogicity in *The Joy Luck Club.*" *MELUS*, Vol. 19, No. 2 (Summer 1994): 99–123.

Amy Tan with Donna Seaman   "The Booklist Interview: Amy Tan," in *Booklist*, October 1, 1990, 256–7.

Veronica Wang   "The Chinese American Woman's Quest for Identity." *MELUS*, Vol. 12, No. 3 (1985): 23–31.

Ben Xu   "Memory and the Ethnic Self: Reading Amy Tan's *The Joy Luck Club*," in *Memory, Narrative, and Identity: New Essays in Ethnic American Literatures.* Ed. Amritjit Singh, Joseph T. Skerrett Jr., and Robert E. Hogan. Boston: Northeastern University Press, 1994.

Index

A

Allman, Karen Maeda, 159
American Journal of Orthopsychiatry, 142
Asia
gender gap in labor forces in, 169
misogyny in, 146–147
Asian/Asian-American women
are not completely accepted in U.S., 164–167
must overcome limiting cultural stereotypes, 144–149
Western myths about, 133–134
The Awakening (Chopin), 9

B

Bisexuality, bicultural identity leads to acceptance of, 150–163
Boelhower, William, 53–54, 55, 57, 58

C

Chao, Elaine, 167
Characters, 19
An-mei Hsu, 43, 57, 129–131
Jing-mei (June) Woo, 42, 43, 44, 45, 49, 51–59, 68, 99, 114–115
Lena St. Clair, 20, 23, 75, 77, 84
Lindo Jong, 46, 57, 62–63, 114, 131–132
Rose Hsu Jordan, 28–29, 31, 67, 76, 131–132
Suyuan Woo, 25–26, 55, 62, 65, 67, 114

Waverly Jong, 43–44, 64, 66–67, 132, 133
Ying-ying St. Clair, 43, 46–48, 57
Chodorow, Nancy, 112, 113, 116
Chopin, Kate, 9
Chung, Connie, 166
Cinderella, 128

D

Daughters
desire assimilation into American culture, 22
mothers are frustrated with failures of, 63–66
reject imposition of matrilineage, 84–85
See also Mother-daughter relationships

E

Eng, David, 158
Ethnic identity
bicultural, acceptance of bisexuality and, 150–163
June's symbolic journey to discover, 51–59

F

Female empowerment, 94–99
through woman-to-woman bonding, 109–119
Feminism, 9
conflict over, replaces cultural conflict, 111–112
is evolving, not dead, 174–181
Ferraro, Thomas, 86

G

"Global Employment Trends for Women 2004," 169

H

Hawthorne, Nathaniel, 7
Hom, Alice, 158
Hunt, Linda, 42
Hurston, Zora Neale, 9

I

Immigrant women, as stereotype, *The Joy Luck Club*'s opening myth rejects, 100–108

J

The Joy Luck Club (Tan)
  Asian-American gender stereotypes in, 120–126
  breaks with stereotype of the passive Asian woman, 10–11
  central "project" in, 59
  daughters damaged by mother's expectations in, 60–69
  female empowerment in, 94–99, 109–119
  feminist ending of, 117–118
  generational differences in, 42–43, 133
  inspiration for, 28–29
  is not strictly autobiographical, 35–39
  maternal line of descent dominates, 80–87
  opening myth of, rejects immigrant women as stereotype, 100–108
  reception of, 23–24
  storytelling reconciles mothers and daughters in, 70–179
  structure of, 18–20

K

Kingston, Maxine Hong, 81, 93, 119, 123
Kinsley, Claire Huang, 150
Kwan, Michelle, 166–167

L

Labor force participation, gender differences in, 169
Lin, Maya, 166

M

McConnell, Mitch, 167
Men
  dominance claimed by, 175
  in labor force, women vs., 169
  as supporting characters, 11
  unemployment among, 170
Metaphors
  mah-jong game as, 82
  spatial structure as, in June's story, 52–54
Mother-daughter relationships, 61–62
  final reconciliation of, 85–87
  as love-hate relationships, 66–67
  in Western fairy tales, 127–129
  women's movement and, 44, 50, 88–93
Mothers
  fear break in genealogical chain, 56–57
  portrayal in *The Joy Luck Club*, 25–26, 29–30
  see themselves as perfected in their daughters, 62–63
  as society's scapegoats, 136–143
  struggle with culture shock, 22–23

P

Professional jobs, women in, 172

Q

"Queen Mother of the Western Skies," 59

R

"The Red Candle," 57
Rescue fantasy, 129–131
Root, Maria P.P., 152
"Rules of the Game," 115
Rust, Paula C., 159

S

"Scar," 57
Schell, Orville, 41
Sciachitano, Marian M., 161
Seattle Times (newspaper), 167
Snow White, 128, 129
Somavia, Juan, 169
Stereotypes
Asian-American gender, in *The Joy Luck Club*, 120–126
cultural, Asian-American women must overcome, 144–149
immigrant women as, *The Joy Luck Club*'s opening myth rejects, 100–108
of the passive Asian women, *The Joy Luck Club* breaks with, 10–11
Storytelling, reconciles mothers and daughters, 70–79
Symbols/symbolism, 72–73
jewelry as, 131
June's trip to China as, 51–59, 87
of maternal authority, 74

the swan story, 96–97, 104
of wind, 132

T

Takagi, Dana Y., 158
Tan, Amy, 10
displaces cultural conflict with feminist conflict, 111–112
June as alter ego of, 99
life of, 16–24
turns autobiography into powerful fiction, 25–34
Their Eyes Were Watching God (Hurston), 9
Themes
of classic Chinese stories, 127
discovery of ethnic identity, 51–59
matrilineage, 80–87
separation/abandonment, 129, 133

U

Unemployment rate, gender differences in, 170

W

Walker, Alice, 119
Wang, Veronica, 49
Williams, Teresa Kay, 162–163
Wirth, Linda, 172–173
The Woman Warrior (Kingston), 81, 82, 86, 93, 123
Women
in labor force, men vs., 169
more are in workforce but job equality is elusive, 168–173
unemployment among, 170

serious literature, as recent
trend, 9
See also Asian/Asian-
American women; Daugh-
ters; Mothers

Women's movement, 9
achievements of, 174–175
mother-daughter relationships
and, 44, 50, 88–93